Heidegger, Art and Politics

Heidegger, Art and Politics

The Fiction of the Political

PHILIPPE LACOUE-LABARTHE

Translated by Chris Turner

Basil Blackwell

First published in French as *La fiction du politique* © Christian Bourgois, Paris
English translation first published in 1990

Basil Blackwell Ltd
108 Cowley Road, Oxford, OX4 1JF, UK

Basil Blackwell Inc.
3 Cambridge Center,
Cambridge, Massachusetts 02142, USA

British Library Cataloguing in Publication Data

A CIP catalogue record for this book is available
from the British Library.

Library of Congress Cataloging in Publication Data
Lacoue-Labarthe, Philippe.
  [Fiction du politique. English]
  Heidegger, art, and politics: the fiction of the political/
Philippe Lacoue-Labarthe; translated by Chris Turner.
    p. cm.
  Translation of: La fiction du politique.
  Includes index.
  ISBN 0-631-16702-1 — ISBN 0-631-17155-X (pbk.)
  1. Heidegger, Martin, 1889-1976—Views on national socialism.
2. National socialism. 3. Political science—Philosophy—
History—20th century. I. Title.
B3279.H49L26 1990   89-35837
193—dc20   CIP

Typeset in 11 on 13pt Bembo
by Footnote Graphics, Warminster, Wiltshire
Printed in Great Britain by T. J. Press Ltd, Padstow, Cornwall

The pain which must first be experienced and borne out to the end is the insight and the knowledge that lack of need is the highest and most hidden need which first necessitates in virtue of the most distant distance

Heidegger, *Overcoming Metaphysics*

Contents

Preface

This short book was not originally intended for publication. These were simply the additional or supplementary pages that are required of one before one can obtain a *doctorat d'État* on the basis of published work. About a hundred pages were required, I was told, in which I should assemble in a few theses – indeed in a *thesis* – what I had managed to put forward in my work as a philosopher. In the process of writing, however, things took a quite different turn: what should have taken the form – more or less – of a 'settling of accounts with myself' has assumed the no doubt daring (or pretentious) proportions of a 'settling of accounts with Heidegger'. There is a very simple explanation for this: I only entered philosophy – if indeed I have entered it – after experiencing the impact or shock (*Stoss* is the term Heidegger uses in 'The Origins of the Work of Art') of Heidegger's thinking. At almost the same time – just a few months later in fact – I learned that Heidegger had been a member of the Nazi party. And I must admit that, like many others, I have never quite got over that fact. In other words, whatever admiration I did – and still do – feel for Heidegger's thinking, I have never been able to come to terms politically – and more than just politically – with that Nazism. This little book attempts, in short, to explain why.

A first version of this text – which was in fact published in a limited edition by the *Association des Publications près les Universités de Strasbourg* – has been circulated in various quarters. Some of the chapters have also been read or presented in various public gatherings. At these various presentations, and also in the discussion occasioned by the defence of my thesis in February 1987, various questions have been put to me and objections raised. This new version attempts to take these into account and, where possible, to respond to them.

July 1987

Acknowledgements

As well as Pierre Aubenque, Lucien Braun, Jacques Derrida, Jean-François Lyotard, Suzanne Saïd and George Steiner, I would like to thank Charles Alunni, Alain Badiou, Françoise Dastur, Alexander Garcia-Düttmann, Jean-Joseph Goux, Gérard Granel, Eberhard Gruber, Werner Hamacher, Daniel Joubert, Sarah Kofman and Pierre Rodrigo.

1

The Age's Modesty

These pages do not in all rigour claim to be philosophy.

This is a question, initially, of the most elementary modesty: what entitles me or gives me the right to claim to be a 'philosopher'?

Let us, however, leave aside anything that has to do with individual cases. Or the merely anecdotal.

The modesty I am speaking of ought to be that of the age, which decidely lacks modesty more than any other: if we contemplate what has been established and deployed in the name of philosophy, what, in such a deployment, has been represented by the appearance of that which the tradition has recognized as philosophies and what the act of philosophizing has, in each case, signified and implied, how could it be other than derisory today to claim still to be engaging in philosophy or – worse – to proclaim oneself a philosopher?

The thing certainly still exists: it is taught and learned; it is spoken and written in the type of discourse that has been its own according to the rules it has established; it is defended – as it should be – when a 'modernism' even more arrogant than the present pretention to philosophizing (though one that is perhaps more clear-sighted about the reality of the situation and the immediate interests of the age) is planning its disappearance from our schools. But if the thing still exists, it does so now only as a tradition; and as a tradition that is now closed. Where today can one see a work of any kind of thinking (i.e. whatever its origins, field and scope) which can be called a philosophy? And in the space academic usage nominally reserves for philosophy, which is indeed itself already counted among the 'human sciences', where can one see the possibility of a philosophy emerging or even the possibility of observing the act of philosophizing taking place? It is from a necessity inscribed in the age – which does not mean a necessity recognized by the age – that the word philosophy now only designates the commentary on philosophy, or where it claims to free itself of this, merely a more or less brilliant and coherent form of epigonal variation. The work of incontestably the greatest thinker of the age belongs almost entirely to the sphere of commentary, and by his own admission, he did not produce a 'work' in the sense in which the tradition has understood the term. On the other hand – the argument is necessary in case someone should seek to blame the dead weight of academic constraints for this – the last two great philosophies in the history of philosophy – the works of Marx and Nietzsche which themselves, already, were not works in the proper sense of the word, were elaborated outside the University. This matter has nothing to do with institutions: philosophical work-lessness begins with Schelling, or even with Kant if one conceives a work in terms of a 'system'. Nearer to our own day, an *oeuvre* like Husserl's in spite of – or rather because of – its claim to be a 'science', doubtless is not, properly speaking, a philosophy. And it is outside the University or on its fringes both that a doubly epigonal counterfeit version has noisily arrogated to itself the title of 'philosophy' and that thinkers of a quite other rigour and a quite other sobriety have continued to put being-able-to-philosophize to the test at its limit (Benjamin and Wittgenstein, Bataille and Blanchot for example).

The modesty I speak of here does not of course signify any form of disavowal of philosophy, nor any kind of scorn for the University as an institution, at least to the extent that this institution does not surrender the restless, questioning attitude it needs to maintain. Modesty is the recognition of a limit. In my case, I might be tempted to say it is 'personal' for a whole host of reasons that are perfectly clear to me, but I know in fact that it is nothing of the sort and that it also affects all my contemporaries, whatever their powers of thought, the scope of their knowledge, their talent for invention, their conceptual virtuosity, the elevated nature of their views or their giftedness as writers. This limit is the limit of philosophy: not a limit fixed by external boundaries or assigned to it, nor one imported from elsewhere, but the limit against which philosophy has itself run up, the limit it has encountered within itself.

This is why the recognition of the limit does not oblige one to give up philosophy, any more than it obliges one to repudiate it. This appeal for modesty is not an invitation to leave philosophy; even less is it a call to be rid of it, as one might lay down a burden and 'move on to something else'. We are not in any way released from philosophy. We cannot pass beyond the limit, or what Heidegger called the 'closure'. We are still living on philosophical ground and we cannot just go and live somewhere else. This does not mean that there is not by rights a place beyond the limit, but that, viewed from here, or in other words from philosophy itself, that place beyond, though always half-glimpsed, is strictly inaccessible. It is as much as we can do, at the very limit, supposing that we can arrive at this point and stay there, to make out or sense its outer edge as a negative image. But in reality, as is shown by everything that has sought to be 'transgressive' in recent years, the limit acts as a screen, and a screen that is too opaque or too reflecting. With the result that even the dizzying, furtive glance at the other edge remains forbidden.

The fact is that the limit here is an effective limit, not simply a frontier or a dividing line. The limit is the limit of the possible. At the beginning of philosophy or, in other words, in the initial indication that being and thinking are the same and that that 'same' is the site of truth, there was a store of possibilities: the determinations of thinking, which is to say, in each case, an interpretation of Being or, if one prefers, an experience of what is (*das Seiende*). Successively adopted in sequence in an order which owes nothing to chance but a great deal to the stage-by-stage emancipation of the sciences each in its own particular rhythm, and to the domination of a 'critical' concept of truth, these possibilities which we have to imagine from the beginning as finite in number, have been exhausted – and this has occurred ever more rapidly and precipitately since the West has entered what it has itself called its modern age. This exhaustion is not a recent

thing. It became apparent at the very point when philosophy
began to question itself, in the tension that constituted it as such,
the meta-physical tension. Or, in other words, from the moment
when, after the thesis on being, in which philosophizing has its
essence, had irreversibly become thesis on being as thesis, all the
theses which succeeded it – whatever the style or the aims of the
most recent great philosophies (accomplishment, restoration,
overturning, liquidation or transcendence of philosophy) – have
been engulfed in the will to a thesis in which has more and more
clearly manifested itself the impossibility of any thesis other than
the thesis, thus condemning the will to desire nothing other than
its own thesis. Since this has coincided with the emancipation, by
a regular process, of the sciences which might concern the thetic
instance in general, be they sciences of the subject or of man,
through which has been accomplished the scientific domination
over the totality of the essent, philosophy has been left with
nothing, no domain of beings, that has not already been taken in
charge by techno-science on the basis of a position on being that
has already arisen within philosophy itself. That is why it would
be no overstatement to describe the sight of the philosophical pose
loftily reasserting itself today as 'derisory': it is and can only be a
mere tinkering around in inessential and subordinate matters
(ethics, the rights of man etc.), journalistic socratism or anthropological approximations. It is nothing that has to do with the
work of thought.

Philosophy is finished/finite (*La philosophie est finie*); its limit is
uncrossable. This means we can no longer – and we can only – do
philosophy, possessing as we do no other language and having not
the slightest notion of what 'thinking' might mean outside of
'philosophizing'. This pure contradiction defines an impossible
situation; and in actual fact the limit is, here, as far as philosophy is
concerned, that of its possibility. It is for this reason that neither
adjuration nor renunciation are appropriate.

What then does this modesty mean, this claim not to be
philosophizing?

This perhaps: no longer desiring philosophy, and desiring
nothing other. The modesty would reside in a paradoxical – and in
itself necessarily contradictory and 'untenable' – suspension of the

will: in a manner, so to speak, of obstinately continuing to philosophize (what is involved this time is an elementary resistance to the vexatious invasion of the 'anything goes') whilst accepting also that one may allow oneself to relinquish philosophizing. When Adorno spoke of accompanying metaphysics in the moment of its fall, there was still – leaving out of account a justified solidarity with philosophy – something 'voluntaristic' in the very grandeur of the gesture. However, quite apart from the fact that, where metaphysics is concerned, the word 'fall' does not seem entirely appropriate (the ruin of the Ideals of Reason in no way prevents metaphysics from continuing to reign in the guise of techno-science and its world – if it is a world), it is precisely the voluntaristic *habitus* that we must renounce. Relinquishment in this sense is will without will, will no longer willing and no longer willing itself, abandoning itself and letting itself be disarmed. A very obscure imperative, going beyond or falling short of the mere refusal of what is dominant, commands that we let philosophy collapse within ourselves and that we open ourselves up to that diminishing, that exhaustion of philosophy, today. We must no longer have the desire to philosophize.[1]

Such a relinquishment assuredly calls for a 'disposition'. But it has little to do with a decision since it is in reality what is imposed upon us by the age. All that might arise from a decision is a certain 'rectitude' towards the age. And yet one knows only too well that the decision to maintain this rectitude is nothing in itself if it is not given to us beforehand to recognize the demand of the age and if, above all, it is not given to us not to falter before that demand.[2]

Recognize here means to recognize that something has happened, and is still happening, which forces relinquishment upon us. An event. And this event, we must admit, is historical in the strongest sense, i.e. in the sense that it does not simply arise from history, but of itself makes history, cuts into history and opens up another history, or else unmakes all history. Such an event is what has occurred in – and as – the first half of this century, of which the second half, somewhere between parody and nightmare, is merely the shadow. We would also have to take the measure of that event. And measure it not on a small scale, taking in the past three or four centuries (the modern age only): Renaissance and Reformation, *Aufklärung* and Romanticism, the speculative accomplishment and destruction of reason, the discourse of emancipation and ideologies of domination. But, since the very possibility of philosophy itself is involved, we must take the true – but incalculable – measure of the whole of Western history. And this is a quite other affair.

NOTES

1   This is in no way to sanction the complacent notion of *pensiero diebole* introduced by Vattimo and Rovatti a few years ago, nor even less is it to accept the obliging catch-all category of the 'post-modern'. The claim not to philosophize makes no compromises whatever with nihilism, however seductive it may seem (but what is the nature of its seduction, in fact?) and the renouncing of the voluntaristic *habitus* necessarily maintains itself in the form of a heroism in the *modern* sense of the term, which is indeed that of Baudelaire or Benjamin, for example. This means that it is, in effect, a resistance that is involved.

2   It is this gift which expresses itself today in the responsibility of another kind of writing. Philosophical writing, with all its norms – amongst which those of the 'philosophy book', paper or treatise are most prominent – has itself reached its limit and has also become exhausted. At least since Romanticism, it is in the possibility of presentation that philosophy has been dealt a serious blow. But, since Romanticism, no other possibility of presentation has offered itself. There is certainly no 'literary' possibility, since this is patently overdetermined by philosophy. There is no other possibility except that possibility apparently without possibility that is interruption, suspension, fragmentation or extenuation. Hence work-lessness. But let us remind the Moderns – and their desire – that precisely such a work-lessness has been at work from the very beginning of philosophy. Perhaps, indeed, it always has represented the hyperbolic idea of the *oeuvre*: the *fatum libellorum* of with Nietzsche spoke is the absolute consummation of their ruin. That is why these pages too, in their non-pretention to the philosophical, lay claim without too

much difficulty to the title of essay or indeed the dissertation –
genres, if there is such a thing, which the Institution does not
condemn and which for that reason, force upon us a responsibility,
but a disarmed responsibility (*une responsabilité désarmée*).

2

Heidegger's Affair

This quite other affair was, as we know, in its time, Heidegger's affair. In what has gone before the reader will also have recognized certain major Heideggerian themes, beginning with that of the 'end of philosophy'. And it was clearly Heidegger who was being referred to in the anatomasis, 'incontestably the greatest thinker of the age'. The rhetorical figure, which was no doubt a little overblown, was none the less intended to signify that there is no thought since Nietzsche's which has delved so deeply and extensively into the question of the essence of philosophy (and, as a consequence, of the essence of thought) nor any which has opened up a dialogue of such scope and rigour with the tradition (with the West).

In this regard, however, I must make one thing clear: to subscribe, as I do, to Heidegger's theses (and in particular to his theses on philosophy), or even to accord his thought such a place (the foremost) cannot in any way be seen as a declaration or profession of what is called 'Heideggerianism'. There are at least two reasons why this is the case. (Since it is fashionable today to denounce the aforementioned 'Heideggerianism' wherever one imagines one has found it, a relatively full explanation is necessary here.)

The first reason is that the very idea of a 'Heideggerianism' is strictly meaningless. Heidegger was neither being coquettish nor inconsistent when he maintained – as he always did – that 'there is no philosophy of Heidegger'. This statement clearly indicated that the question that was his – in short the question of Being – could in no case produce a new thesis on Being nor, even less, give rise

to any 'conception of the world'. The delimitation and deconstruction (*Destruktion, Zerstörung, Abbau*) of philosophy (of ontology) do not constitute a philosophy, not even a philosophy of
philosophy, nor, to borrow an expression from Kant, who was
admittedly for a time Heidegger's guide, a 'metaphysics of
metaphysics'. And if *Sein und Zeit* could still pass – once the
anthropological misinterpretation had been set aside – for the
search for a 'basic ontology', it is perfectly well known that from
1935 onwards Heidegger explicitly and definitively renounced the
very term 'ontology'. To object, as some have done, that the
question of Being – which, in passing, is indissociable from the
very project of deconstruction – is somehow an 'invention' of
Heidegger's and in some way arises from a 'choice' that is his
alone, or simply from his philosophical 'position', cannot remotely
be regarded as serious: not only does Heidegger take into account
the whole of philosophy since its origins; not only does he base
himself upon the various declarations of 'accomplishment' (Hegel)
or 'overcoming' which have arisen *within philosophy itself* (so that it
is from *philosophy itself* that he receives the question of the end of
philosophy), but we know by his own admission that it is also
from philosophy, via Brentano and the Husserl of the sixth of the
Logical Investigations that he receives the question of Being. From
all philosophy, if one works back from the most paradoxical
manifestations of 'forgetting' (Nietzsche: being is an 'empty
word', a mere 'vapour'; Hegel: being is the 'indeterminate immediate') to the anxiety felt by Plato barely moments after the
very first beginnings. That is, if one goes back – and here we have
before us the dazzling opening pages of *Sein und Zeit*– to the *aporia*
to which Sophistes 244a on the question of the meaning of the
expression 'essent'★ bears witness. And if one were to go on to say
then that all this is simply a matter of 'point of view' and that
Heidegger does not in the least take account, for example, of
ancient materialism, the Sophists, British empiricism or analytic
philosophy, what has one added which Heidegger, starting out

★The original German term is 'seiend'. I here use Ralph Manheim's translation,
'essent', though elsewhere I have also followed the usage of Macquarrie and
Robinson who distinguish between 'being' or 'what is' (*das Seiende*) and
'Being' (*Sein*) [translator's note].

from the question of *philosophy*, that is from an unshakeable allegiance to the initial definition of philosophy, has not already precisely delimited as a regional and subordinate point of view? That philosophical discourse may unfold itself upon the basis of an ontological thesis which has not been made explicit is something Heidegger has never denied (he demonstrated this brilliantly with regard to Marx for example). But this was obviously not what solicited his attention within philosophy.

To be or call oneself 'Heideggerian' therefore has no meaning, no more than to be or call oneself 'anti-Heideggerian'. Or rather both mean the same thing, namely that one has missed the essential point in Heidegger's thinking, and one is condemned to remain deaf to the question which the age poses through Heidegger. There are, inevitably, Heideggerian theses, to which one may choose to subscribe or not. But these theses do not form themselves into a philosophy, except in the weak sense of the word. Similarly, and this is just as inevitable, Heidegger maintains a philosophical *gestus* and in large part Heideggerian discourse is articulated in the language of philososphy. But this is still not a philosophy, unless one were quite dishonestly (though such dishonesty is commonplace nowadays) to reduce Heidegger's theses to theses from the philosophical (e.g. Hegelian) tradition, in feigned ignorance of the incommensurability that exists, by definition, between a thesis on being and the question of being.

On the other hand – and this is a second reason for not claiming to be 'Heideggerian' – one has frankly to acknowledge that Heidegger himself was not able to prevent such a 'Heideggerianism' becoming possible. He even consciously encouraged it, especially after 1945 in France, authorizing by his actions the philosophical (and even ideological) take-up of his thought and therefore certain of the objections which were themselves philosophical to that possible philosophical interpretation of his thought (not all: Adorno's critique, even in its violence and injustice, often succeeds in hitting the mark because Adorno knows what is involved in the question of the end of philosophy, and sees with clarity where Heidegger betrays himself. The same cannot be said of the stodgy Marxisant or sociologising attempts at settling scores nor of the dubious operations I referred to immediately above).

Beyond what is none the less not merely anecdotal (the role played by Beaufret, and, in particular, by his students; the opening up of French universities after the war to the German tradition), this phenomenon – the birth and implantation of a 'Heideggerianism' in reality finds its explanation in Heidegger himself. The fact is that, on two occasions at least, Heidegger, by his own choice, indulged in philosophy.

A first time, massively, and in a way that was, all in all, absurd (moreover, he knew this and he spoke in private of the 'greatest act of stupidity' (*die grösste Dummheit*) of his life)[1] on the precise occasion of his political commitment of 1933–4.

A second occasion, but this is probably merely the other side of the same coin, when he used the writings of Hölderlin and, to a lesser extent, of Trakl to take a step beyond strict questioning or the simple heralding of 'another kind of thought', and produce the first outlines of that 'other kind of thought.

Both these failures to live up to the original exigency are not of the same style, nor did they have the same consequences. Even though there is no doubt – and this is something I shall come back to – that his 'Hölderlinian' preaching is the continuation and prolongation of the philosophico-political discourse of 1933. But they certainly are failures in that, on each occasion, Heidegger does precisely what he calls on Jünger not to do, i.e., he 'crosses the line' whether that line be conceived in Nietzschean – Jüngerian terms as a 'line of nihilism' or 'zero meridian', or whether it be thematized more broadly as 'closure' of metaphysics or philosophy. Now, as Heidegger himself showed, such a crossing unfailingly re-introduces what it claimed to pass beyond. Heidegger himself, no doubt, did not elude the implications of this same logic.

How? The question is a difficult one: what one can detect in Heidegger that is philosophical clearly does not consist in the positive or thetic part of his discourse (once again the position or thesis would have to be of – or on – Being, and this is out of the question). It does not consist either in its 'ideological' dimension, even if reduced to phraseological effects or to idiomatic choices and therefore implying if not ontic 'valorizations', then at least ontic preferences (but all the essents privileged by Heidegger, the home (*Heimat*), the path or way, the thing, the language etc., resonate with that *unheimlich* tremor which 'makes strange' the familiar, stable, well-known entities they seem to be; and, most importantly, what kinds of pre-suppositions, themselves philosophical, permit the production of a concept like that of 'ideology'?).[2] It is not even certain that the philosophical can be detected in the various resistances Heidegger sometimes erects against what he has himself set in train in the name of deconstruction: in a relic of humanism, for example, or a sort of nostalgia for presence (the problem posed by nostalgia is not simple and his deconstructive vigilance is only rarely found wanting). Where then is it to be detected?

My hypothesis is as follows: it lies, on the one hand, in the tenor and style of the commitment of 1933 which are precisely (because it is a commitment that is involved) philosophical, and as a consequence produce statements that are philosophical in type and can be located as such in the tradition. The commitment of 1933 is founded upon the idea of an hegemony of the spiritual and the philosophical over political hegemony itself (this is the theme of a *Führung* of the *Führung* or of the *Führer*) which leads us back at least to the Platonic *basileia*, if not to Empedocles. His statements (on Germany, on work, on the University etc.) are purely and simply programmatic and are, moreover, organized in a number of 'Appeals'. On the other hand, if it is true that certain of these statements (the most immediately political or the least distant from the National – Socialist programme) will subsequently be unequivocally abandoned and repudiated, in its deepest intentions and the essential nature of its aspirations, the injunction of 1933 will be maintained to the end. Admittedly, after the war it will cease to be addressed – explicitly at least – to Germany, and will be addressed to Europe or the West. None the less, from 1934 to the end, taking into account the inflection caused by the collapse of the Third Reich (and also Heidegger's withdrawal, both naive and cunning, from *Öffentlichkeit*, from that light of 'publicity', which 'obscures everything') it will be considerably amplified, from the *Beiträge* to the final developments of his thinking on Hölderlin, until it produces, along the lines of a model which it is impossible not to identify with the Romantic model of Jena, a 'new mythology', albeit one which is inscribed – with all the requisite vigilance – in negative. (But all the same, the *Gevier* and the 'lack of sacred names', the ring (*ring und gering*) of the world and the four,★ the waiting for a new god and a host of other themes of the same order all make up a mythology in the philosophical sense of the term, (i.e. without apocalypse of the name or reputation of the place.) There is no possible appeal against Beckett's fearsome phrase which Adorno had the perspicacity to place as an epigraph to one of the most justly harsh essays he devoted to the Heideggerian reading of Hölderlin, 'It is easier to raise a shrine than bring the deity down to haunt it'.[3].

It might be thought then that we have before us here, hastily sketched out, all the elements required for a 'critique', of Heidegger. But this is not the case at all. From where might one 'criticize' Heidegger? From what 'point of view'? This much, however, is true: recognition of the importance of his thought – or indeed unreserved admiration for it – in no way excludes infinite mistrust. Not of the thinker himself (Heidegger was right to invoke, as he often did, Valéry's adage: 'Qui ne peut attaquer le raisonnement, attaque le raisonneur'[4]) but of what his thought entails or carries with it, what it sanctions and justifies. This comes back to saying that the situation with Heidegger is just as impossible and hardly more 'tenable' than it is with philosophy. I shall try to explain why this is the case.

In the event, it is not recognition nor even admiration which poses a problem, but mistrust. Or the intrication of recognition and mistrust. Why mistrust? (Given that it is not a question, as Habermas suggests, borrowing a remark of Heidegger's on Nietzsche, of 'thinking *with* Heidegger *against* Heidegger'.)

The answer is a brutal one: on account of Heidegger's *political* attitude. It is on this that the discussion (in German, *die Auseinandersetzung*) must bear.[5]

★On the 'four' and the 'fourfold', see 'Building', Dwelling, Thinking' in Heidegger, *Poetry, Language, Thought* (New York, Harper and Row 1975), pp. 145–61).

NOTES

1 Quoted by Heinrich W. Petzet in his Preface to Martin Heidegger – Erhart Kästner, *Briefwechsel* (Insel Verlag, 1986), p. 10.

2 This is why all the denunciations of the Heideggerian idiom (by Adorno, Minder, Faye, etc.), though they may be politically apposite and confirm his affinities with some particular lexicon within the general National Socialist movement, such as Swabian agrarianism for example, never manage to avoid the trap of counter-ideology. To espouse Marxism against Heidegger has always been to miss the essentials of his thought – including his political thought.

3 *The Unnamable* (London, Calder and Boyars, 1959), p. 346.

4 'Autre Rhumbs', *Tel Quel, Oeuvres II* (Paris, Gallimard, 1960), p. 685. Heidegger's translation, which occurs in the correspondence with Kästner cited above, runs '*Wer das Denken nicht angreifen kann, greift den Denkenden an*', (p. 83): 'He who cannot attack the thinking attacks the thinker'.

5 I have tried to begin this work of 'discussion' in two essays published in *l'Imitation des modernes* (Galilée, 1986): 'La transcendence finie/t dans la politique' and 'Poétique et politique'. Certain very allusive analyses here refer to these two essays.

3

The Political

The answer 'On account of Heidegger's *political* attitude' is a
(philosophically) brutal one, because it takes no account of the
Heideggerian delimitation of the political (I use the term 'the
political' here to translate the Greek '*ta politika*' and indicate the
essence of things political). This is true. But there was none the less
a political act on Heidegger's part, with its (inevitable, accepted
and acknowledged) dimension of compromise, and there was also
a profound commitment which he was never later to disown
(neither, so far as we know today, in the professorial allusions or
declarations after 1934 nor in any of the three texts left behind at
his death[1]). And, above all, apart from these aforementioned
compromises – and others – this *political* act corresponds exactly to
the meaning Heidegger attributes to the word and, when the said
act is articulated in discourse, it is articulated without any apparent
difficulty in the language of Heidegger. When he says in 1935 that
to translate *polis* by State or City 'does not capture the full
meaning' because 'The *polis* is the historical place★, the there *in*
which, *out* of which, and *for* which history happens', then instead
of speaking confusedly of 'ontological disavowal' (which hardly
makes any sense), we would do better to see this attempt to define the
essence of the political as what best illuminates *a posteriori* the style
and argument of 1933. The same is true when, in the lectures of 1936
on 'The Origin of the Work of Art', Heidegger ranks among the
number of the institutions or the historial theses of *alētheia*,
alongside the work of art, the nearness of the god, authentic

★In the French original, Lacoue-Labarthe renders Manheim's 'place' as 'historial
site' [translator's note].

sacrifice and thought's questioning, the 'founding of a State'. It is clear that, for Heidegger, 'political', in the sense in which he became politically committed, means 'historial' and that the act of 1933, having regard to the University, but also, beyond it, to Germany and to Europe, is an act of foundation or re-foundation. And it is no less clear that in 1933 National Socialism embodied that historial possibility or at least it was the bearer of it. The famous phrase from the lecture on the 'Introduction to Metaphysics' on the 'inner truth and greatness of this movement' has no other meaning.

That is why the commitment of 1933 is neither an accident nor an error.

It is not an accident because – apart from the fact that it is deliberate and motivated – one cannot really say, re-reading the texts, that it is unexpected or absolutely surprising.[2] As far as strictly university politics is concerned, the *Rectoral Address* advances nothing that was not already included in the Inaugural Lecture of 1929. And as for general politics, that is to say, as for History, the essence of what was proclaimed in 1933 had already been said in *Sein und Zeit*, as may be seen in division 2, chapter 5. Admittedly, it was not with the destiny of Germany that these paragraphs were concerned, nor with the (re)commencement of the Greek commencement. But the positive reference to the Nietzsche of the second of the *Thoughts Out of Season*, a text that is itself extremely political, together with the overall tenor of the undertaking, entirely founded upon repetition (*die Wiederholung*) in the sense in which that concept is elaborated in the book on Kant, already implied that the question of the spiritual destiny of the European West and the historial re-foundation of Germany be thought, when the appropriate moment presented itself, in the same terms

And if anyone is surprised by Heidegger's 'revolutionary radicalism' in 1933 (and have we not heard a rumour, of late, that Heidegger in fact felt quite close to the SA and is reputed to have publicly shown hostility to the ideologues officially supported by the SS: Rosenberg, Krieck and Bäumler?[3]), then let them re-read the proceedings of the Davos Colloquium of 1929. When Heidegger, speaking to Cassirer, said: 'This nothingness must not be a cause for pessimism and melancholy, but must lead us to understand that there is only genuine reality where there is resistance and that it is philosophy's task to snatch man from a life that would be limited to using the works of the mind and snatch him from that life to throw him back up [in a way] against the harshness of his destiny',[4] what is this but a foretaste of the tone of 1933? Contrary to what has been said in a number of places, Heidegger's commitment is entirely consistent with his thought. And the 'political' and the 'philosophical' were so interwoven that practically all his teaching from the so-called 'turn' (*Kehre*) up until 1944, was devoted to a 'settling of accounts with' National Socialism, which in reality reveals *a contrario* the truth which Heidegger had perceived in it or believed in all seriousness ('Not that I spoke for the sake of mere appearances – I saw this as the one possibility', see ' "Only a God can save us": The Spiegel Interview', in T. Sheehan, *Heidegger, the Man and the Thinker* (Chicago, 1981), p. 49) that he had perceived in it. That such a belief should have given rise to a properly philosophical act – the act which one might call, mixing the two languages that are at bottom implied by the act itself, an act of *archi-Führung* – is not the product of some accident that has happened to 'thought' but reveals what constantly threatens the said 'thought' – its danger. Which is less, as Heidegger will write in 1947, 'the bad and thus muddled danger' of 'philosophizing' than the danger 'which is the evil and thus keenest danger', i.e. thinking itself. For, he added, '[thinking] has to think against itself, which it can only seldom do'.[5] There is a great temptation – and I have myself given in to it on occasion – to impute the commitment of 1933 to a failing or a sudden loss of vigilance or even, more seriously, to the pressure of a thinking as yet insufficiently disengaged from metaphysics. But this is to forget that metaphysics, at least in the form of that ineradicable *Trieb* recognized by Kant and Nietzsche is at the most secret heart of thought itself. 'Thought', if there is such a thing, can never proclaim itself 'disengaged' from metaphysics. And this, moreover, is what always leaves it *'engagé'* in this world, however great its prudence or its disillusionment.

This, it seems to me, is the reason why we cannot speak of error either. There would have been an error if Nazism, whatever its 'reality' in other respects, had not borne within it the possibility

Heidegger saw there. Now manifestly it bore that possibility, at least in certain of its features, with respect to the destiny of Germany and that of the West. The distress (*Not*) which underlies the National Socialist insurrection, as it underlies Heidegger's protest in the *Rectoral Address*, is not simply the economic vortex into which Germany is sinking and the collapse of the Weimar Republic that followed defeat and the Treaty of Versailles, i.e. the outcome of the first and inaugural 'total mobilization' in Western history; nor is it simply the disarray of a Germany which has known for over a century that it has received the spiritual heritage of the whole of the West and which knows equally well that it cannot for all that arrive at existence as such, condemned as it is either to remain painfully in abeyance or to find itself crushed in the 'vice' formed by Russia and America (referred to in the *Introduction to Metaphysics*) that holds Europe in its grip and, in Europe, holds in its grip the people in the 'middle' that is the German people; it is also, and perhaps even principally the anxiety and even the dread arising from the acknowledged exhaustion of the modern project in which the catastrophic Being of that project stands revealed. No requirement of rhetorical emphasis forces Heidegger to invoke, at the heart of his *Rectoral Address*, Nietzsche's phrase, 'God is dead': this phrase exactly expresses the situation, i.e. 'the forsakenness' (*Verlassenheit*) of 'man today in the midst of what is'.

In 1933, Heidegger is not mistaken. But he knows in 1934 that he has made a mistake. Not about the truth of Nazism, but about its reality. The 'movement' remained deaf to his solemn injunction (his address has turned into *maladresse*) and the movement has shown itself to have achieved precisely what Heidegger saw it as being called upon to fight against: not only the compartmentalization of the University under the constraints and imperatives of professionalization (without, it need hardly be said, the slightest questioning of the essence of science), nor even just what such an academic politics was more than merely a symptom of: the impossibility of an historial decision in the face of the collapse of the historical possibilities and the pure and simple continuance, beneath a grandiloquent and authoritarian bluster, of the old world (after all, is it not true that Nazism for a time 'put Germany back on its feet' and managed to make 'function' what so-called democracy had hardly even been able to keep under control, without disrupting either the economic or political logic – or both these logics – of the modern project? How else is one to explain the *eagerness* of practically the whole of the financial and industrial bourgeoisie, and the fundamentally *conciliatory* attitude of practically all the Western 'democracies'?); but, and this is more fundamental, it had achieved that nihilism itself within which and as which 'the encounter between planetarily determined technology and modern man' cannot arise.

It might be said then that it is correct to speak of error, or at least, of illusion. This is true if it is meant in the sense in which Granel intends it when he speaks of *mirement* (Littré describes this as a sailing term: 'an effect of refraction which makes an object seem higher than it really is': Thought is only refracted (*se mire*) in reality – which is not its role, but may become its inclination – by inducing in its turn a sort of '*mirement* ' or doubling-up. This is what happens to the National Socialist movement throughout the *Rektoratsrede*. In the eyes of thought, it is reduced to a kind of pure matter without any specific forms of its own, and thus becomes susceptible of being 'taken over' [an allusion to the derisory strategy outlined by Heidegger in the *Spiegel* interview] at the same time as also being elevated on the horizon to the heights of possibilities that are not specifically its own, but with which it is imagined it can be invested'.[6]

It is true again, then, in this sense: Heidegger overestimated Nazism and probably wrote off as merely incidental certain things which were already in evidence before 1933 to which he was, in fact, staunchly opposed: anti-semitism, ideology ('politicized science') and peremptory brutality. But – I shall also add – who in this century, in the face of the unprecedented world historical transformations that have taken place, and in face of the apparent radicalism, whether of 'right' or 'left' of the various revolutionary projects, has not been duped? And in the name of what? 'In the name of democracy perhaps?' Such things can be left, I think, to Raymond Aron, to the official philosophy of Capital (of the achieved nihilism for which in effect anything *goes*). But what of those who were great figures in their respective ways? I cite at

random Hamsun, Benn, Pound, Blanchot, Drieu and Brasillach
(I do not except Céline whose writing none the less I find over-
rated). Or, in the other camp, Benjamin, Brecht, Bataille, Malraux
(I do not except Sartre, whose moral authenticity is quite beyond
question). What did the old world have to offer them with which
they could have resisted the irruption of the so-called 'new world'?
From this point of view, all things considered, the merit of
Heidegger will have been to have succumbed for only ten months
to this Janus-headed illusion of 'new times'.

In this sense, which has, all things considered, *become* banal, it
will always be possible to speak in terms of error. But I contend,
or maintain, that we are not dealing here with an error once we
take into account the idea that Heidegger, and behind him the
whole of the German great tradition (Marx, in part, included), had
of the historic destiny of the West – though it must, it is true, be
admitted that Heidegger speaks of the *historial* destiny which
makes more than a negligable difference. It is not an error, but a
consequence. And if that consequence had as its consequence,
even if for only a period of ten months, *consenting to* Nazism – to
something of that order – then we must speak not of committing
an error, but of *doing wrong [faute]*.

NOTES

1   Apart from the famous (and disappointing) interview published by
    Der Spiegel immediately after his death (31 May 1976, vol. 30, 23),
    there exists the request for reinstatement addressed to the University
    authorities in 1945 (Cf. Letter to the Rector of Freiburg University:
    'An das Akademische Rektorat der Albert-Ludwigs-Universität') and
    the text he entrusted to his son Hermann, also in 1945, that was
    meant to be included in a possible posthumous republication of the
    Rektorats-Rede or 'Rectoral Address' (Martin Heidegger, *Die Selbstbe-
    hauptung der deutschen Univeristät – Das Rektorat 1933/34* (Kloster-
    mann, 1983), translated by Karsten Harries as 'The Self-Assertion of
    the German University', *The Review of Metaphysics* 38, 3, 151
    (March, 1985), pp. 467 – 80. A fourth document, a 'Letter to the
    Chairman of the De-Nazification Committee at Freiburg Universi-
    ty', which also probably dates from 1945, adds no further details.

2   Heidegger insists a great deal on the fact that he had never
    before been preoccupied with politics and that he was still hesitating
    on the very morning of his election about his candidature. But it is
    obvious that if hesitation there was – and this is plausible – it was
    caused essentially by the heavy burden of responsibility that would
    clearly be involved, for one so ill-prepared for the management of an
    administration and unused to political negotiation. As for his pro-
    fessed prior 'apoliticism', this has the same value as any apoliticism at
    a moment when politics is in fact breaking down, and the spectre of
    the totalitarian 'everything is political' is raising its head. The terrible
    thing about political 'innocence' is that it is always possible that it
    may go over *immediately* into the worst of its opposites and that, *of
    itself*, it always belies in advance its alleged purity. Hitler was, of
    course 'apolitical'. It is true, however, that in the testament left to his
    son, Heidegger writes: 'What made me hesitate until the very last day
    to assume the rectorate was the knowledge that with what I intended
    I would necessarily run into a twofold conflict with both the "new"
    and the "old". The "new", meanwhile, had appeared in the form of
    "politicized science" [*politische Wissenschaft*: Francois Fédier explains
    that this term refers in National Socialist ideology to 'militant
    science'; in other words, it was 'one instrument among others in the
    struggle between the "races" for world domination'] the very idea of
    which rests on a falsification of the essence of truth. The "old" was
    the effort to remain responsible to one's own "specialty", to help
    advance it and to utilize such advance in instruction, to reject all
    reflection on the foundations of science as abstract-philosophical
    speculation or at most to admit it as unnecesssary decoration' ('The
    Rectorate 1933/34: Facts and Thoughts', *Journal of Metaphysics* 38, 3,
    151 (March, 1985), pp. 482–3. (Translation modified to take account
    of sense of German verb *laßen* and of particular usage of the adjective
    politische in this context – translator's note.) One must not, in fact,
    under-estimate the seriousness and profundity with which the prob-
    lem of the University was confronted by Heidegger, from *What is
    Metaphysics?* through to the *Rektorats-Rede* and beyond (on this point,
    which is decisive, see Gérard Granel, 'Pourquoi avons-nous publié
    cela?', in *De l'Université*. TER, Paris, 1982).
3   Still in the same testament, Heidegger writes 'I had no illusions about
    the possible consequences of my resignation from office in the spring
    of 1934; after June 30 of the same year [date of the 'Night of the Long
    Knives', notes Fédier, on which Hitler set about physically eliminating
    Röhm and his SA], these consequences became completely clear.

Anyone who after that still assumed an administrative office in the university was in a position to know beyond the shadow of a doubt, with whom he was bargaining'. (The Letter to the De-Nazification Committee at Freiburg University is almost identical in its wording.) This statement is ambiguous: is it the *massacre* that opens his eyes to the real nature, i.e the brutality, of the regime; or is it the disappearance of the SA 'tendency' which causes him to lose all hope in the movement's 'possibilities'? At a textual level, it is difficult to see how one could decide between the two readings, but this in no way constitutes a proof. In the matter of revolutionary radicalism, however, the dialogue with Jünger is much more illuminating. Granel notes that in the *Spiegel* interview, Heidegger situates himself 'amid the general confusion of opinion and political tendencies' of the Weimar period as a man in search of a 'national, and, above all, social attitude', to use his own words. He quotes Naumann and Spranger, not Jünger himself. Need we, however, recall that if Jünger felt strictly political affinities, it was more with the 'National Bolshevism' of his friend Ernst Niekisch than with the 'vulgar' National Socialism with which he refused from the outset to have any truck whatever, or from which even, in the words of Louis Dupeux, 'he turned away in horror' (Louis Dupeux, *Stratégie communiste et Dynamique conservatrice* (Honoré Champion, Paris 1976); see his discussion of 'Ernest Jünger et le national-bolchevisme', in *Le Magazine littéraire* 130 (November, 1977). One may also consult, though with more circumspection, Hermann Rauschning's *The Revolution of Nihilism* (New York, Arno Press, 1972)). The difference between the two nationalisms, the Bolshevik and the Socialist, is not simply between the aristocratic and the popular. What truly divides them is the question of race. Heidegger's aversion to the racist ideology and biologism of the Nazi theorists, to be seen on many occasions in his post-1934 teaching, reflects this crucial division (Charles Alunni points out, however, that in *Entscheidung*, which appeared in Berlin in 1930 (Widerstands Verlag), Niekisch's argument is openly anti-semitic. The Jews are ranked among the *westlerisch* (Western) element which is to be eliminated – something the Bolsheviks have achieved to perfection in the case of Trotsky. 'It is in a feverish process of untold vehemence that this self-purification is accomplished.' One could hardly, in fact, be clearer. We should note, however, that Niekisch does not lapse into *völkisch* ideology: Lenin, for example, is honoured with the title of *asiatischer Mischling* (Asiatic half-caste).

4   Ernst Cassirer, Martin Heidegger, Davos Colloquium. Heidegger uses the verb *benutzen*, 'to use', which can also be understood as 'profit from' or 'exploit'. In an as yet unpublished essay ('Levinas en France', 1986), Alain David interprets this declaration as an anti-semitic *topos*, corroborating in this regard the famous (and contested) testimony of Frau Cassirer. And Henri Declève had already proposed the following translation: 'Philosophy has the task of throwing man back on to the harshness of his destiny by making him abandon the dubious persona of a man who is happy to draw utilitarian profit from the works of the mind' ('Heidegger et Cassirer interprètes de Kant', *Revue philosophique de Louvain* (November, 1969). What is in any case certain, and here again there is copious evidence of this in his teaching, is that Heidegger harboured a definite aversion for the world of culture, the 'intellectuals' and the university 'establishment' (as is attested by the famous phrase in the *Rectoral Address*, which itself is not without anti-semitic connotations: 'For spirit (*Geist*) is neither empty cleverness, nor the noncommittal play of wit (*Witz*)), nor the endless drift of rational distinctions, and especially not world reason; spirit is primordially attuned, knowing resoluteness toward the essence of Being' (p. 474). An aversion which connects with what he felt towards *urbanity* in general, on the basis, as is well-known, of his attachment to his native soil, to the peasant world, to solitude etc. (cf. *Warum bleiben wir in der Provinz*, translated as 'Why do I stay in the Provinces?,' (1934), in Thomas Sheehan (ed.), *Heidegger, the Man and the Thinker*, (Chicago, Precedent, 1981), pp. 27–30). In the 1930s, however, this pathos, which will assume a quite benign form after the war, is accompanied by an 'heroic' pathos, Nietzschean in style, which sets the tone not only of his political proclamations but also of his teaching (an example would be the paragraph devoted to 'the figures of the worker and the soldier' in the Lectures of 1941 on the *Grundbegriffe, Gesamtausgabe* (Frankfurt/Main, Klostermann, 1981), vol. 51, pp. 35–9). It will be recalled that it was this heroic tone and this radicalism of argument that had struck Hannah Arendt at Marburg ('Martin Heidegger at Eighty', *New York Review of Books*, 17 (21 October 1971), pp. 50–4).

5   'The Thinker as Poet' ('*Aus der Erfahrung des Denkens*'), *Poetry, Language and Thought*, trans. A. Hofstadter (New York, Harper and Row, 1975), p. 8.

6   Granel,' Pourquoi avons-nous publié cela?', p. 105

♦

Postscript

Géard Granel takes me to task in his analysis of the *Rectoral Address*
(with which, in the main, I agree) for having identified – or rather
aligned – the language Heidegger used in 1933 with the political
language traditionally employed by philosophy, from Plato to
Hegel. (The object of his attention here is my essay, 'La transcendence finie/t dans la politique', now included in *L'Imitation des
modernes* (Galilée, Paris 1986), pp. 135ff. Here is what Granel
writes:

> However, before going on to that reading [of the *Rectoral Address*] in
> which not only the 'present' of the 1930s but also our own is at issue,
> we have to examine one last question which, in the 'vigilant'
> commentaries that the *Rectoral Address* has caused to spring up in
> France in recent days, still masks our access to it. That question is
> that of *the permanence, or the resurgence of the metaphysical form* in the
> very heart of the only thinking that has taught us to discern the
> fundamental features of such a form and to attempt the 'step back'
> from it. The suspicion – legitimate in itself – consists in supposing
> that the *mirement* of National Socialism on the horizon of late
> modernity, or alternatively the illusion of an 'immediate resonance'
> of thought in present events, might entail an existential-historial
> relapsing into the classic traps of the relation between philosophy
> and politics. In other words, the shadow of Plato and Hegel would
> still hang over the *Rectoral Address*.
>
>   One cannot, in my opinion, grant this point to the exegetes–
> censors of the 1933 text, even if one admits that this is the one
> subject on which their contributions have been most interesting.
> One cannot simply turn the 'Führer' of the speech's opening all of a
> sudden into 'Führer und Hüter' (guides and guardians) and then read
> the Heideggerian re-routing of the 'Führerprinzip' into 'geistige
> Führung' (spiritual guidance), and the reference to the spiritual
> mission of Germany into 'existence in knowledge' in the Greek
> sense, as evidence that the problematic of the *Rectoral Address* is the
> last avatar of Platonism. It is not good enough either to associate this
> theme of knowledge with the State form in order to turn Heidegger
> into the reincarnation of Hegel. Between Heidegger and the great
> metaphysical thinkers with whom efforts have been made to align

him, there are at least two *essential* differences concerning knowledge and a no less essential distance between them so far as the
question of the State is concerned.[1]

There is a misunderstanding here, or else I have expressed myself
badly. Firstly, the point of view of 'vigilance' or, worse still, of
censorship is totally alien to me. I leave all that, as it seems to me
Granel does too, to the political commissars or the preachers of
whatever hue (they are, today, legion – and we all know their
eagerness so well). What I was attempting to say about Heidegger's political texts, in my own way and to the best of my
particular abilities, belongs exclusively under the heading of
polemos, within thought and within the period, and, as a result,
presupposes more than mere respect for Heidegger's thought and
more than attention for the period in which he lived, the period in
which, in many respects, we ourselves are still living.

   Secondly, if I have in fact genuflected towards the theme of
'relapse' into that very thing – metaphysics – which Heidegger's
thought alone 'taught us to discern in its fundamental features'
(which I do not for one moment contest), I did not do so to 'align'
Heidegger's thought on knowledge and the State with philosophical determinations, whether Platonic or Heideggerian, of knowledge or the State. Moreover, I cannot very clearly see how one
might manage to achieve such an 'alignment', though it must be
said that, with regard to the State, Heidegger's commentary on
the *Republic*, as it unfolds in the first volume of his *Nietzsche*, holds
a few suprises.[2] But no more than I confuse the 'Greek beginning'
invoked by Heidegger in 1933 (and, indeed throughout his work)
with the beginning of philosophy as such with Plato or, to use
Granel's terms, of the transmutation of 'Socratic mantic into
psycho-transcendental mathesis', I do not reduce Heidegger's
categories to their (ever possible) metaphysical concepts. When I
mention Hegel, and in particular when I refer to Plato, I confine
myself to speaking of a *similar* 'attitude' or 'gesture', or, if one
prefers, a *similar posture* – taking my inspiration for this from a
remark by Hannah Arendt in 'Martin Heidegger at Eighty' in
which she compares Plato and Heidegger – or rather takes them
both to task – on the grounds of an identical fascinated submission

to the tyrant. I do not know if one can 'align' Hitler and Dionysius of Syracuse. But I observe that there exists a disturbing kinship between the Seventh Letter and Heidegger's testamentary writings and I still hold the belief that *Führung* as Heidegger conceives it is not far removed from Plato's *basileia*, taking into consideration Heidegger's own interpretation of this concept. Here indeed, to support my contention, is that interpretation: the reader will easily recognize in it what the *Rectoral Address* says, though this obviously does not mean that Heidegger thinks Being as Idea:

> *dikè* is a metaphysical concept, not originally one of morality. It names Being with reference to the essentially appropriate articulation of all beings . . . Knowledge of *dikè*, of the articulating laws of the Being of beings, is philosophy. Therefore the decisive insight of the entire dialogue on the State says, *dei tous philosophous basileuein (archein)*: it is essentially necessary that philosophers be the rulers (see *Republic*, Bk V, 473). The statement does not mean that philosophy professors should conduct the affairs of state. It means that the basic modes of behavior that sustain and define the community must be grounded in essential knowledge, assuming of course that the community, as an order of being, grounds itself on its own basis, and that it does not wish to adopt standards from any other order. The unconstrained self-grounding of historical *Dasein* places itself under the jurisdiction of knowledge, and not of faith, inasmuch as the latter is understood as the proclamation of truth sanctioned by divine revelation. All knowledge is at bottom commitment to beings that come to light under their own power.[3]

Lastly, on the question of Nazism, if I grant Granel that it is pointless to go on 'getting indignant about the monstrosity of fascism if we do not ask ourselves what the *monstrum* demonstrates', I do not think it is simply possible to act as if Heidegger's commitment, reduced to the proclamation of the *Rectoral Address* alone, belonged exclusively to the Cause of thought and could therefore be treated with such 'benign consideration'. We know – but this must be re-stated emphatically – that Heidegger refused in the clearest possible manner to give the least sanction to antisemitism and the official racist biologism of the 'movement', even if the *Rectoral Address*, contains this fearful passage (and how might one begin to re-think this?): 'And the *spiritual world* of a people is

not the superstructure of a culture, no more than it is an armoury
stuffed with useful facts and values; it is the power that most
deeply preserves the people's strengths, which are tied to earth and
blood; and as such it is the power that most deeply moves and
most profoundly shakes its being (*Dasein*).' What rector, in fact,
after the re-organization of the universities in 1933 refused to
authorize the display of the *Juldenplakat*? However, Heidegger
knew – as Granel both knows and does not know – that anti-
semitism is not an 'ideological' outgrowth of the movement but
something quite essential to it. It was something with which he
certainly did not compromise himself, but it also did not 'stop'
him. Granel's only note on this matter does not, in my view,
match up to the magnitude of this question *for thought*. Granel's
note relates to a reference to the '"pragmatic" demands of the
National Socialist student organisations':

> It will be said that these demands have many other characteristics
> over and above the ones they derive from such a 'pragmatism':
> racism, for example, and anti-semitism in particular. It remains to
> be seen – taking into consideration what gives German racism of the
> 1930s and 40s the particular coloration of *Hitlerian* madness –
> whether racism has not fed, since that period, and does not even
> today feed upon a characteristic of 'occupations or trades' and even
> of 'plain work' which we have not questioned, which would be that
> occupations and work, though in appearance now universal 'rights',
> are in reality fiercely defended privileges.

There is obviously something in this. But all the same, it makes
little sense to lay all the blame upon unemployment when what is
at stake here is no more nor less than the essence and destiny of the
West. For this is the question posed by 'anti-semitism in particular'.

NOTES

1 Gérard Granel, 'Pourquoi avons-nous publié cela?', in *De L'Université*
  (Paris, TER, 1982). pp. 115–16.
2 *Nietzsche*, vol. 1, *The Will to Power as Art* (London, Routledge and
  Kegan Paul, 1981), pp. 165–9.
3 Ibid., p. 166.

4

Doing Wrong

To speak of *doing wrong* presupposes that there exists an ethics, or at least that an ethics is possible. Now it is probably the case today that neither of these conditions is fulfilled. Firstly because ethics, whatever the most sophisticated or the least simple-minded efforts expended in that direction (I am thinking of the efforts of Levinas), also suffers from the general exhaustion of philosophical possibilities and manifestly cannot claim to stand outside that exhaustion except at the cost of a certain blindness towards it and its origin: how and from where could one *philosophically* get back beyond Heidegger's delimitation of ethics and humanism? Secondly – and I shall come back to this point – because what has occurred this century, for which each day *we* show that we are *a posteriori* responsible, has subjected the very idea of ethics to an unprecedented shock and has perhaps definitively destroyed its foundations. We are, of course, forced to live and act according to the norms and prescriptions of ethics, i.e. norms and prescriptions derived from the old ethical systems, but no one can any longer be in any doubt, unless they wish simply to indulge in re-legitimizing the obsolete, that we are in this regard entirely without resources. It is no doubt still possible to answer the question 'How are we to judge'? It is certainly no longer possible to answer the questions, 'From what position can we judge?' 'In the name of what or of whom?' For what are lacking, now and for the foreseeable future, are names, and most immediately 'sacred names', which in their various ways governed, and alone governed, the space (public or other) in which ethical life unfolded.

This lack of ethical resources is what must, by an extremely obscure and quite undecipherable imperative keep us exclusively within the interrogative mode.

I do not then hazard the words 'doing wrong' with regard to Heidegger from within any form of ethical certainty. I only hazard them because there is the admission, in Heidegger, of being without resources; and because at least on one occasion in his own personal statements, he hinted at an admission of having done wrong, when he spoke in the *Spiegel* interview, of his attitude at the time of Husserl's death, of a 'human failing' (*Versagen*).

What are we to say of such a failing beyond what in actual fact it owed to his personal relationship with Husserl (but not without regard to what the history of the relationship shows)? I have no wish to put Heidegger on trial. By what right could I do so? I want to confine myself to a question – a question for thought. That is why it seems pointless to me to go back again over the facts. Apart from the fact that, for want of adequate documentation, one risks continuing to spread a number of errors, false rumours, or pure and simple slanders, I do not see what effect a recollection of the facts can have on the matter, unless it is simply considered an accepted fact, and beyond question, that being a Nazi was a crime. This is something one may argue politically. I do so myself. But the thing itself still remains to be thought, and, so far as that is concerned, anecdotes are of no help to us, even if there exist documents and testimonies which are, in my opinion, quite damning.[1]

Heidegger's 'wrong' does not therefore consist in the 'compromises' he made with full knowledge of the facts, compromises which indeed he clearly condemned in 1966. Simply by keeping his signature at the bottom – or top – of the *Rectoral Address*, he indicates quite clearly in what respects he disagreed with the regime politically. And he disagreed over almost everything, from the obtuse 'Schlageter line' nationalism to international politics (the question of the League of Nations) and the 'socialist' approach to the question of work, even if he did agree on the need for a national and social revolution. As well as emphasizing what he had always uncompromisingly rejected (displaying the *Judenplakat*, book-burnings, the dismissal of *Dozente* on political or racial grounds, 'politicized science'), he marked out no less clearly just what in his eyes was unacceptlable: and it is patent, whatever might have been said elsewhere, that what was unacceptable was anti-semitism. But the unacceptable did not prevent compromises, and he compromised with a 'movement' for which anti-semitism was a fundamental principle, not the product of some ideological excrescence with which one might choose to agree or disagree. By becoming a member of the Nazi party, however brief and even dignified that participation, one was necessarily committing oneself to a racism. And if one believed it was possible to 'detach' the racism from the 'movement', then one was not simply being blind to the nature and 'truth' of the 'movement', but one thought, or so we must assume, that it was worth putting up with a little bit of racism to see the movement victorious: anti-semitism was simply regarded as an incidental cost.

Speaking of the intellectuals in 1933, of her friends, and of those who had 'their theories about Hitler' ('Fantastic, exhilarating, sophisticated and very high-flown theories, theories above the nature of the usual ramblings'), Hannah Arendt is no doubt right when she says 'These were simply people caught in their own traps [in the trap of their own constructions]. What happened subsequently was not something they had wanted . . . They were . . . only people who occasionally did something for a few months, or, in the worst cases, for a few years: they neither killed nor informed on anyone.'[2] And moreover we know that in most cases, Hannah Arendt forgave them, including Heidegger, as she was perfectly at liberty to do. This is not, however, the question. The question is that the said intellectuals, or at any rate Heidegger, said nothing after the war, publicly and within their own sphere of responsibility – that of thought – when the collapse of the Third Reich revealed what it did. And what it did reveal was in fact *apocalyptic*. Which comes down to saying that the question is that the said intellectuals, or in any case Heidegger, refused to admit that it was ultimately the duty of thought to confront that particular phenomenon and to seek to take reponsibility for it.

And yet Hannah Arendt articulates what an 'abyss' its revelation constituted:

Before that, we had thought that we did indeed have plenty of enemies. But that had been quite natural. Why shouldn't a people

have enemies? This was really something quite different. It is really
as if the abyss opened up before us, because we had imagined that all
the rest could be sorted out in some way or other, as can always
happen in politics. But not this time. This should never have
happened. And I am not speaking of the number of victims, but of
the systematic production of corpses etc. I don't need to expand any
further on this subject. Auschwitz should not have happened.
Something happened there which we still have not come to terms
with.

But it is she herself, speaking of the intellectuals who had not
desired what was to be revealed ten years later, who then adds,
'Consequently, it seemed to me there had to be some kind of
bottom to this abyss' by which she means that in spite of
everything 'things were sorted out with a lot of people'. Once
again she was quite at liberty to do this. But the question remains:
can the silence of certain people, or in any case – in the eyes of
Hannah Arendt herself – of the greatest of them, provide a bottom
for such an abyss? I do not believe so – and this has to do with the
very nature of the abyss.

The only sentence in which, to my knowledge, Heidegger
mentions this abyss is one he pronounced in 1949 in one of the
cycle of four lectures delivered at Bremen on the subject of
technology (this is the only one that remains unpublished, though
it is quoted in Wolfgang Schirmacher's *Technik und Gelassenheit*
Freiburg, (Karl Alber, 1984), and it is also mentioned, though not
actually cited, in Otto Pöggeler's book). It reads as follows:

> Agriculture is now a motorized food industry, the same thing in its
> essence as the production of corpses in the gas chambers and the
> extermination camps, the same thing as blockades and the reduction
> of countries to famine, the same thing as the manufacture of
> hydrogen bombs.

This sentence is scandalously inadequate.

It is not inadequate because it relates mass extermination to
technology. From that point of view, it is indeed absolutely
correct. But it is scandalous and therefore lamentably inadequate
because it omits to mention that *essentially*, in its German version

(though admittedly what nation in Europe did not enthusiastically join in, as France and the lands of *Mitteleuropa* and Latin fascism certainly did), mass extermination was an extermination of the Jews and that this is incommensurably different from the economico-military practice of blockades or even the use of nuclear arms. Not to speak of the agricultural industry ... The fact that Heidegger was not even able, nor probably even wished to state this difference is what is strictly – and eternally – intolerable.

This is so for an extremely *simple* reason: the extermination of the Jews (and its programming in the framework of a 'final solution') is a phenomenon which follows *essentially* no logic (political, economic, social, military etc.) other than a spiritual one, degraded as it may be, and therefore a historial one. In the Auschwitz apocalypse, it was nothing less than the West, in its essence, that revealed itself – and that continues, ever since to reveal itself. And it is thinking that event that Heidegger failed to do.

Why was the West revealed there? That is to say, where is the incommensurable difference between the Extermination and any other technical phenomenon whatever?

One is surely justified in thinking that the Extermination, as a systematic project governed by an ideology, was not something new in Europe. I will not simply speak of the age-old, relentless persecution of which the Jews have been the victims, but of all the mass murders (whatever the number of victims, which is of no interest: there is a mass as soon as there is a collectivity) which were carried out for the sake of an Idea. Since the massacre of Melos which revealed Athenian democracy to itself and sent it into its decline, there is a long list of historical models of Extermination: the destruction of Carthage, the Inquisition, the Counter-Reformation, the revolutionary Terror, the slave trade and colonial massacres, American ethnocide etc. We know that the Angel of History, as Benjamin said, has its face turned towards a pile of wreckage and debris, and that the History of which it is the Angel is that of the West. (But what other civilization has not also been founded upon murder?) These examples, none the less, all have this in common: in each case, the massacre is linked to a situation of war or civil strife; there is a genuinely political, economic or military issue at stake; the means employed are those of armed struggle, police or judicial repression; and the operation is directed by some belief or rationality. And this is still true, whatever the scale or enormity of the facts, of the Stalinist form of the same operation, including Cambodia.

In the case of Auschwitz, things are quite different – despite appearances (powerful ideology, state of war, police terror, totalitarian organization of politics, extensive technological capacity, etc.). For two reasons: the Jews as Jews were not in 1933 agents of social dissension (except of course in phantasy); they did not represent any kind of homogeneous political or religious force; they did not even appear to have any particular social cohesion. At most, one might say, greatly simplifying the problem of assimilation, they formed a religious or historico-cultural minority. But they did not threaten Germany as the Melians threatened the Athenian Confederation or as the Christian heretics or Protestants threatened the State based on divine right, as the Girondins threatened the French Revolution or the Kulaks the establishment of socialism. They were a threat as people *decreed to be* Jews, that is to say as a heterogeneous element, only for a nation that was painfully lacking an identity or existence of its own and which was, in fact, also facing very real threats both internal and external. But it is already sufficiently well-known, I think, that the 'Jewish threat' is something that belongs to the realm of projection.

The second reason is as follows: the means employed in the Extermination were, in the last instance, neither industrial, military, nor those of a police force (this is why Heidegger's statement is absolutely correct). Certainly the police and the army were indispensable: for seeking people out, transporting them, administering the camps and even carrying out some of the killings. But in its 'final' aspect, the annihilation no longer had about it any of the features of the classical or modern figure of systematic oppression. None of the 'machines' invented to extract confessions or remorse or to mount the edifying spectacle of terror, was of any use. The Jews were treated in the same way as industrial waste or the proliferation of parasites is 'treated' (whence no doubt the sick joke of 'revisionism' about the Zyklon B; and yet to say that the Zyklon B served as a de-louser is the best possible 'proof' of the gas-chambers: chemical methods and cremation). That is why the machines used to this end or 'adapted' (but not invented like the Virgin of Nuremberg, the wheel or the guillotine), were the – banal – machines – of our industrial plants. As Kafka had long since understood, the 'final solution' consisted in taking literally the centuries-old metaphors of insult and contempt – *vermin, filth* – and providing oneself with the technological means for such an effective literalization.

This purely hygienic or sanitary operation (which was not only social, political, cultural and racial etc., but also *symbolic*) has no parallel in history. Nowhere else, and in no other age, has such a will to clean and totally eradicate a 'stain' been seen so compulsively, without the least ritual. To speak of a 'Holocaust' is a self-serving misinterpretation, as is any reference to an archaic scape-goating mechanism. There was not the least 'sacrificial' aspect in this *operation*, in which what was calculated coldly and with the maximum efficiency and economy (and never for a moment hysterically or deliriously) was a pure and simple *elimination*. Without trace or residue. And if it is true that the age is that of the accomplishment of nihilism, then it is at Auschwitz that that accomplishment took place in the purest formless form. God in fact died at Auschwitz – the God of the Judaeo-Christian West at least. And it was not at all by chance that the victims of that annihilation attempt were the witnesses in that West of another origin of the God who was venerated and thought there – if not indeed, perhaps, of another God – one who had evaded capture by the Hellenistic and Roman traditions and who thereby stood in the way of the programme of accomplishment.[4]

That is why this event – the Extermination – is for the West the terrible revelation of its essence.

NOTES

1   Among the worst is the report addressed by Heidegger to the academic authorities in 1933 on the subject of a certain Baumgarten, a report which would eventually lead to the expulsion of Baumgarten from the *Dozentschaft*. 'To judge by his intellectual conduct, Dr

Baumgarten probably comes from the liberal–democratic circle that formed around Max Weber in Heidelberg. During his stay here, he was anything but a National-Socialist ... After landing up with me, Baumgarten spent a great deal of time with the Jew Fränkel, who was previously employed at Göttingen and has since been removed from his teaching post here. I suppose that, once launched on this course, Baumgarten ended up at Göttingen; hence his current contacts there. For the moment, I consider it out of the question that he should be admitted either into the SA or into the body of university teachers.' Labelled a *Judengenosse*, Baumgarten would in fact be expelled from the *Dozentschaft* (quoted by Hans Saner, publisher of Karl Jaspers, in *Notizen zu Martin Heidegger* (Munich, Piper, 1978). Eberhard Gruber informs me, however, that this same Baumgarten, after having been re-admitted into teaching, obtained his *Habilitation* (university teaching qualifications) in 1935 and taught philosophy at the University of Königsberg from 1940 to 1945. In the event, he had been allowed simply to submit a written declaration stating that he had never met Professor Fränkel (*Notizen*, p. 5; see also the article by E. Baumgarten, in Klaus Piper and Hans Saner (eds.), *Erinnerung an Karl Jaspers* (Munich, Piper, 1974), pp. 123–46). As his attitude in 1945 indicates (he pronounced a *Schuldrede* at Göttingen and declared himself *in extremis* close to the conspirators of 20 July 1944) and also his polemic with Jaspers on Nazism as 'total evil', we may suppose that Baumgarten was not, in fact, himself a wholly spotless character. This does not, however, in any sense mitigate the odious nature of Heidegger's action (his statement is not an expression of his professional opinion, but a denunciation), which, it must also be said, was not the only one of its kind. It is reported – and the statements on this tally and seem plausible – that he also wrote a report of the same type on Max Müller, one of his most brilliant – and most faithful – students. When asked after the war why he had seen fit to inform the authorities that Max Müller was not 'for the regime', Heidegger replied – with either unfathomable naiveté or infinite cunning – 'Because it was true'.

(One may consult the testimony of Max Müller on 'Martin Heidegger, ein Philosoph und die Politik', in the *Freiburger Universitätsblätter*, Heft 92 (June, 1986), Rombach Verlag, pp. 13–22. It seems also that one may rely upon the testimony of Karl Löwith, which is free of hatred, but equally damning: *Mein Leben in Deutschland vor und nach 1933, Ein Bericht*. (J. B. Metzler, 1986), especially pp. 32–45 and 56–9. It goes without saying that the volume of personal testimonies and information seems destined to increase. Elizabeth de Fontenay, in an article published by the *Messager européen*, vol. 1 (1987) ('Fribourg – Prague – Paris. Comme l'être, la détresse se dit de multiples manières'), cites a number of other examples given in N. Blondel-Parfait's thesis, *Théorie pratique, Histoire d'une erreur* (University of Paris I, 1986). And the researches in Germany of Hugo Ott and Bernd Martin are well-known. The work of the historians has in fact hardly begun. I doubt, however, that it will be able to contribute anything really decisive: it is not in Heidegger's minor (or major) compromises, nor even in his declarations and proclamations of 1933 to 1934, that the crux of the matter – philosophically – is located.)

2   From the text of a television interview by Günter Gaus, broadcast by the German Channel II on 28 October 1964. [My translation, C. T.]

3   These four lectures, delivered under the heading, *Einblick in das, was ist*, are partially published in the brochure *Die Technik und die Kehre* (Pfullingen, Neske, 1962).

4   That God died at Auschwitz is clearly what Heidegger never *said*. But everything suggests he could have said it if he had wanted, that is if he had agreed to take a certain step which is, perhaps, that of courage. (I can, perhaps, understand why he refused to say anything to those who, wielding their 'rights' as victors, were demanding explanations and accounts of his conduct. But I shall never understand why he said nothing to those survivors, such as Celan for example, who *looked to him* for some kind of statement.) In the testament of 1945, after referring to the thinking of Jünger on domination and the figure of the worker, Heidegger writes 'From the vantage point of this reality of the will to power I saw even then what *is*. This reality of the will to power can be expressed, with Nietzsche, in the proposition: 'God is dead'. Essential considerations led me to cite this proposition in my Rectoral Address. The proposition has nothing to do with the assertion of an ordinary atheism. It means: The supersensible world, more especially the world of the Christian God, has lost its effective force in history. (See my lecture, 1943, on Nietzsche's word 'God is dead') [translated by William Lovitt in M. Heidegger, *The Question concerning Technology and other essays* (New York, Harper and Row, 1977), pp. 53–112]. Had things been different, would the First World War have been possible? And even more, had things been different, would the Second World War have become possible?' And, a few lines later, referring to the history of the Nazi period, Heidegger

pronounces the word *Unheil*, which is the German word for radical evil, disaster, total loss of grace: 'Those who even then were so endowed with the gift of prophecy that they foresaw all that came, as it came – I was not so wise – why did they wait almost ten years before opposing the threatening disaster (*Unheil*)?'

5

The Caesura

I propose to term such an event a *caesura* in the sense Hölderlin accorded this term.

We know that, for Hölderlin, the structure of tragedy possesses an order and, for that reason, is calculable. The governing principle of this structure is that of alternation (*Wechsel*) or the rhythmic succession of representations (*Vorstellungen*). Hölderlin gives the name 'representation' (within which he also includes feeling and reasoning) to the mode in which a tragic hero, that is, the 'whole man', defined in Kantian terms as a 'system of receptivity', develops upon the stage 'insofar as he is under the influence of the element', i.e. of the divine. This alternation or this exchange of representations gives its status to the tragic *agon*, to what Hegel will describe as the conflict between the two divided powers of ethical substance. For Hölderlin, however, agonal exchange ('all is discourse against discourse') tends more towards equilibrium than mere succession. Not, as Hegel thinks, because neither of the contending forces can win out over the other, but, he says, because 'the tragic *transport* [in French in the original] is, in truth, strictly empty, and as devoid as possible of connections'. And he adds:

> Thus, in the rhythmic succession of representations through which the *transport* is (re)presented (*sich darstellt*), what in metrics is called a caesura, the pure word, the counter-rhythmic interruption, becomes necessary to counteract, at its acme, the turbulent succession of representations, in such a way that it is not now the succession of representations that appears but representation itself.

From the formal point of view, this definition of the caesura poses no difficulties whatsoever. If tragedy is a rule-governed *agon* between two representations of the divine, an *agon* which becomes aggravated (as is marked in each 'scene' by the transition to stichomythia and, in the overall structure of the tragedy, by the 'rise to extremes' and if the law (*Gesetz*) in tragedy is, rather, the law of equilibrium, then the caesura – the counter-rhythmic suspense – is structurally necessary to guarantee that equilibrium. This means that the moment of the caesura is the moment at which the truth of the conflict of representations appears as such: representation then appears 'in itself'. And Hölderlin points out that in the two Sophoclean tragedies which he analyses in this way, *Oedipus Rex and Antigone*, the caesura occurs each time at the point where Tiresias intervenes, though this occurs at different stages (the beginning or the end) according to the type of tragedy (modern or ancient) which each of the two plays represents. He explains that this is because Tiresias: 'makes his entry into the course of destiny like the seer who can see into the force of nature [*Naturmacht*: another name for the divine] which, tragically, snatches man from his sphere of life, at the median point of his inner life, and carries him off to another world, the eccentric sphere of the dead'.

The caesura, Tiresias's intervention (and the 'remedy' to the aggravation of the *agon*), can therefore only be explained by the nature of the tragic 'transport', which is a snatching away, a carrying off, a pure ecstasy which consigns the man 'under the influence of the element' (of the God) to the 'eccentric sphere of the dead'. And in fact,

> The (re)presentation of the tragic rests, principally, on the fact that the monstrous [*das Ungeheure*] – how god and man join together and the power of nature and the innermost being of man boundlessly become as one in fury – is to be understood through the boundless becoming-one being purified by boundless separation.

Here again, it is not too difficult to recognize a – metaphysically transposed – echo of Aristotelian *catharsis*. Through the death of the hero, tragedy represents the infinite separation of that pure monstrosity or enormity (*hubris*) that is the infinite collusion of man and God, their 'joining together' and their 'becoming-one in fury'. Hence the specific effect of tragedy is to 'purify' the 'empty transport' of enthusiasm. The lesson of tragedy is rigorously Kantian, and, consequently, Judaic in its form ('Kant is the Moses of our nation'): to man defined as 'system of receptivity', the *intuitus originarius*, the strictly meta-physical 'transport' is forbidden. Commenting upon a fragment of Pindar, to which he gives the title, *The Law [Das Gesetz]*, Hölderlin writes: 'The immediate . . . is impossible for both mortals and immortals . . . But rigorous mediateness [*Mittelbarkeit*] is the law.' It is this law which founds and governs tragedy. It may be called the *Law of finitude.*[1]

In tragedy, but also in history, of which tragedy is more than emblematic (in reality it is its structural matrix or, alternatively, the tragic Law is historicity itself), the law of finitude takes the form of the 'categorical turning away (*kategorische Umkehr*)' of the God, which renders *imperative* for man a turning back toward the earth. A moment of limitless separation, therefore, which 'caesuras' God and Man, who from that point on, 'so that the course of the world should have no lacunae in it, and *the memory of the Heavenly Ones should not be extinguished, communicate in the all-forgetting form of unfaithfulness* for divine faithlessness is best preserved [*behalten*: to retain in memory]'. And, in fact, it is the Law itself.

This is how Hölderlin presents this paradox of faithful infidelity – of the respect for the Law – which is imposed by the very logic of tragedy, which is always an infinitely paradoxical logic (an infinite paradoxicality):

> At such a moment, the man forgets himself and the God, and turns around, admittedly in a holy way, like a traitor. At the extreme limit of suffering [*Leiden: pathos*], nothing indeed remains but the conditions of time or space.
>
> At this point, the man forgets himself because he is entirely within the moment; the God forgets himself because he is nothing but time; and both are unfaithful, Time because at such a moment it undergoes a categoric change and beginning and end simply no longer rhyme within it; man because, at this moment, he has to follow the categorical turning away and that thus, as a consequence, he can simply no longer be as he was in the beginning.[2]

This text really requires a long commentary. I shall, however, merely draw from it the following points. First, at the height of

the tragic suffering, the *pathos* – in other words at the moment
when man suffers and endures the God – 'nothing remains but the
conditions of time or space', in other words, *nothing*, if space and
time are 'conditions' in the Kantian sense, 'pure forms' or 'empty
forms', prior to their being assigned any possible content'.[3] The
tragic 'moment' is an empty or zero moment – the moment of the
very nullity of the immediate – a pure hiatus or a pure syncope, a
'counter-rhythmic interruption of the course or succession of
events'. The God presents himself immediately as the abyss, the
chaos of his withdrawal. This is why, in a note that precedes the
Anmerkungen, Hölderlin had defined the (re)presentation of tragedy as that unique (re)presentation in which 'the sign = 0'. And
we must note that this moment, which is a moment of 'forgetting'
– of the God and of oneself – is the condition of possibility of all
memory and all (faithless) fidelity, that is to say, the condition of
possibility of all thought. Second, faced with this immediate
withdrawal of the immediate, this 'categorical' turning away
which is, purely and simply, the *catastrophe*, man must imperatively
submit. In the genuinely Greek form of tragedy, this submission
immediately takes the form of death. The destiny of Antigone:
'The God presents himself in the figure of death'. In the 'modern'
form of the tragic, on the other hand (and this is what I am
referring to here), submission is the acceptance of mediateness, or
in other words, of finitude. The destiny of Oedipus – the figure of
the excess of knowledge (the 'eye too many') – which is also our
destiny (for Hölderlin, as for many others, the West is Oedipal) is
'wandering beneath the Unthinkable'. [This is Lacoue-Labarthe's
translation *'errance sous l'impensable'* of *'unter Undenkbarem wan-
deln'* – translator's note.] In this case, however, destiny follows
from the fact that once the God, i.e. Time (in the translation of
Antigone, Zeus is called the Father of Time) has turned away in re-
volt – and this is the tragic cut, the advent of nothingness, the pure
event – beginning and end no longer rhyme, and the man who is
to succumb to this fate 'can no longer be as he was in the beginning'.
And Hölderlin adds: 'This is how Haemon stands in Antigone.
And Oedipus himself in the middle of the tragedy of Oedipus.'
The scansion of the tragedy thus opens up a temporality that is
both irreversible and discordant (or out of tune): what follows the

caesura will never be the same as what went before; the end will never again resemble the beginning. The 'caesura-ed' man literally does not *rise up* again, does not *recover* (*ne s'en* relève *pas*).

For Hölderlin (as for Hegel, but at a quite other level), Sophoclean tragedy was the 'testament' of the Greek experience of the divine, that is to say, the document attesting to the necessary withdrawal of the divine. By this token, as for Hegel too (at least the Hegel who is not yet Hegelian), it held the secret of historicity, if the destiny of history is nothing other than erratic accomplishment of the Law of finitude (and there, as everyone knows, Hölderlin probably has nothing more in common with Hegel). In these conditions – it little matters whether this lies outside Hölderlinian 'theology' or not – it is not perhaps impossible to raise the caesura to the rank of a concept, if not *the* concept, of historicity. A caesura would be that which, within history, interrupts history and opens up another possibility of history, or else closes off all possibility of history. But two points absolutely must be made here:

1 We may only speak of a caesura in the case of a pure event, i.e. an empty or null event, in which is revealed – without revealing itself – a withdrawal or the nothing-ness (*né-ant*).
2 There is a caesura only where an attempt at immediacy (an excess) is interrupted or cut off, i.e. a crime against the – historial – Law of finitude.

In the case of Auschwitz – which Blanchot calls that 'event without response' – these two conditions are, as the sinister-sounding phrase has it, 'satisfied'. And this is so for the only time, I believe, in modern history (this is why Auschwitz opens up, or closes, a quite other history than the one we have known up until now.) With one small proviso – though this changes everything – that Auschwitz is the site of a dissociation: those who suffer the 'categorical turning away' in the unprecedented figure not even of death, but of a mere purging (an unutterable degradation of *catharsis*) – are not those who desired immediacy or committed a crime, but those upon whom those who did do these things literally discharged themselves (once again, an unutterable degradation of

catharsis – making of Auschwitz, no less literally, the *discharge* of
Germany (and of Europe). I cannot comment on the 'theological'
meaning, if there is one, of Auschwitz (though the 'silence of
God', more merciless even than his withdrawal, seems to me to
exceed all that human *pathein* can endure). All I can say is that
Auschwitz belongs to a sphere beyond tragedy, at once more and
less than tragedy: more, because the infinite separation is absolutely
hyperbolic: less, because no (re)presentation of it is possible and
Auschwitz is, very precisely – and I shall return to this – the
useless residue (*le déchet*) of the Western idea of art, that is to say,
of *technē*.

This is, unfortunately, what Heidegger, who knew a good deal
about the caesura (what else, after all, is the *Ereignis*?) and
Heidegger alone can enable us to understand, he who obstinately
refused, however, to acknowledge Auschwitz as the caesura of
our times.

NOTES

1 This is why, like every work (*oeuvre*), tragedy is calculable. The
   principle and justification of this calculation are the Law itself. It is
   stated as follows at the beginning of the *Anmerkungen*:
   'Amongst men, one has particularly to take into consideration in
   relation to every thing, that it is a something, that is to say, that it is
   something knowable through the means [*Mittel*, for which Hölderlin
   gives the French equivalent *moyen* in brackets] of its manifestation
   [*Erscheinung*], that its mode of conditioning may be determined and
   learned.'
2 Hölderlin, *Anmerkungen*, Section 1, *Gesammelte Werke* (Frankurt/
   Main, Insel Verlag, 1969), p. 730
3 On this point, see Jean Beaufret, *Hölderlin et Sophocle* (Paris, Gérard
   Monfort, 1983).

Postscript

I must now reply to several objections to which the thoughts developed above have given rise. Though these come from various different sources, they intersect and, in a certain sense, converge.

The first thing that is said to me is: why make such a unique event, such an exception out of Auschwitz – and the Extermination? There have been, will be and are other Auschwitzes; Auschwitz is only one among the innumerable wholesale massacres which, as a result of the deployment of technology, recent history has produced in increasing numbers, and made systematic. No specific difference, in terms either of the choice of victims or of the means employed, enables us to single out Auschwitz. In the end, then Heidegger is right about this.

This first objection arises for two different series of reasons.

On the one side, the point is made that the 'singling out' of Auschwitz in reality secretly re-introduces by the back door the anti-semitism it was supposed to combat (all the more so in that I do not mention either the gypsies, the homosexuals, the mentally defective or the Communists etc.). This is the argument which sees philosemitism as merely the reverse of anti-semitism, and, as such, to be regarded with great suspicion as its possible symptom (as was recently made very clear to Maurice Blanchot). This argument is accompanied by another, which I do not, I hope, misrepresent, if I condense it in the following terms: if one is trying to avoid the racism one is combatting, is there any sense other than theologico-political, if not, indeed, purely and simply theological (or, worse, 'mystical') in 'assigning central importance to' the Jews alone in this way, when there were other victims? And, from this perspective, the references I make to the death of God or the historial interpretation of the tragic caesura are contested (my 'vision of history' is dubbed not merely 'idealist', but catastrophic–mystical).

From another side, I am told more simply that the camps, whether or not they were equipped with gas-chambers, are only one of the forms – not even a figure – never mind, a spectacular one – of technico-capitalist exploitation and that, as such, they are in no way exceptional. By placing myself among the 'Extermina-tionists' (the category is, apparently, the opposite of the 'Revision-ists'), I am said to be perpetuating the self-interested manoeuvre of the various propaganda-machines, East and West, which have been only too eager to denounce the evils of Nazism, barbarism or sundry devilish abominations the better to conceal or minimize their own misdeeds (massacres and deportations, torture, ruthless exploitation of the Third World etc.) which are in reality of the same nature as the Extermination.

Presented in this way, I find it futile to submit this objection to discussion, since I cannot bring myself to find it acceptable. That is to say that:

(1)   From the very point of view I have taken up (a debate with Heideggerian reflection on History, but one *conducted in the terms of that reflection*), I cannot see what logic other than a 'spiritual', 'historial' one governed the Extermination. The Extermination is, if you will, the product of a pure metaphysical decision and one inscribed, moreover, in the very heart of National Socialist doctrine. This does not mean that I deny its technological charac-ter in the sense Heidegger gives to this term (I quite explicitly say the opposite). And it does not mean either that, detaching it from other logics (economic, military, political etc.), I consider it illogical or irrational. It means, in fact, and this is the point of the discussion, that when one thinks History in terms of the deploy-ment of metaphysics, and one calls on the West, under this same heading, to face its responsibility – which Heidegger never ceased to do – one cannot maintain silence on the massacre of the Jews, in so far as it is precisely the massacre of *the Jews*. The man who was able to tell his students and listeners in the summer term of 1936 that the work of Spinoza was not 'Jewish philosophy' but a Cartesian philosophy (which was a courageous act at the time) was also able, when the time came, and no doubt better able than others, to take the measure of the Extermination as a 'spiritual' and 'historial' event. I am trying therefore, in spite of him, but also because of him, to take such a measure and to ask myself of what consequence this will manifested to eliminate the 'Jewish

element' is for the irrevocably Graeco–Judaeo–Latin West itself. We knew that there existed a centuries-old anti-semitism (with an essentially religious basis). We knew that Western man was a killer (in fact he is not the only one, but he had succeeded in equipping himself with unrivalled means to kill). We even knew – or could guess – that the West had always hated something in the Jew. Could we guess that Western man was going to fulfil himself in what he proclaimed to be his truth, in himself and for himself, in this calculation and planning of the murder of those whom he decreed, with contempt for the most elementary evidence, did not belong to the West, or were sapping it from within?

(2) It was precisely so as to avoid any 'exterminationist pathos' that I did not speak of the other victims of the massacre, whose fate, though it follows from the same exterminationist logic (and I concede without difficulty that from this point of view Nazism is in no way exceptional), does not follow from the same 'symbolic' logic, if I may employ this term. This does not mean that horror is somehow at its height if the victims are European petty-bourgeois like you or me (technological mass extermination is always the height of horror, or worse) nor that the Jews have some greater importance (whether historical, 'cultural' or ethical etc.) than, for example, the Gypsies. In considering such murders – and in terms, therefore, of pain – I do not see what sense there would be in according special importance to anyone at all. But it does mean that the *metaphysical significance* of the murder is not the same. Once again genocides or attempted genocides, exterminations of enemies, whether internal or external, eliminations of social 'elements' considered 'noxious', whether overt or covert, ritualistic or scientific, are legion in history and Nazism created nothing new in this regard. One can even find 'futile' massacres, ones that were gratuitous or absurd. And a whole range of others which are a product of metaphysical or religious fanaticism. But the invention of the 'Jewish question' in modern Europe on the basis of the fulfilment of the Western ideological project (techno-science), without motives of a religious nature – or indeed any other nature, a point to which I shall return – and the 'treatment' of that question on the same basis, are of quite a different scope. Marxist

'science' in no sense demanded of Stalin that he deport the Crimean Tatars, nor that he order the Katyn massacre (in his conception of it, it did perhaps demand the Gulag, but the Gulag and its millions of dead is not Auschwitz). The 'science' from which National Socialism claimed inspiration, and behind this, the idea it had of Europe and the West do, however, directly lead to Auschwitz. There is no 'philosemitism' in such a statement, and it is not reintroducing some shameful or insidious anti-semitism by the back door to confront, at least within thought (I was going to say that the rest is my concern, but this is not even true), a question which Europe and not only Germany (but Germany above all) has 'put on the agenda'. And has done so, I believe, irreversibly.

(3)   Since my critics grant that the idea of a political or social, or indeed cultural, 'Jewish threat' is a product of phantasy or invention, I maintain that not only the choice of victims (according to their belonging to the alleged 'Jewish race') but the means employed for their elimination have no relation with those in the counter-examples that are raised against me. The loathsome discussion of the gas chambers must not lead us to forget that there was not the least economic justification for 'concentration', nor that the camps of which Auschwitz is emblematic were intended for extermination not production. When 'Marxists' make Auschwitz out to be just another case of modern capitalist exploitation (on a world scale) with no qualitative difference from the massacres this century has organized (and is organizing now) in the name of exploitation, this violent, systematic 'reduction' (a quite disgraceful one when you look at who profits by it) lacks all rigour and does a disservice to the cause it claims to support. (It is true that the same people deny any fundamental difference, in this regard, between the two variants of capitalism, state-capitalism and the liberal form, or between the regimes or political forms that are more or less superimposed upon them: Stalinism, fascism, dictatorships and democracies.) I accept that Extermination has been exploited for political ends. But that is no reason to refuse to analyse it in its specificity. I repeat: Heidegger's phrase, in so far as it characterizes Extermination as a technical phenomenon, is

'absolutely correct'. But technology, as he knew, cannot be regarded as a mere transformation within the register of pro- duction or exploitation (Heidegger also spoke in 'Overcoming Metaphysics' of man as having become 'raw material'), nor as a change of scale in armaments production: whatever was written over the gate at Auschwitz, it was not a labour camp, except in the official fiction, and the gas chambers and the ovens were not weapons.

(4) Lastly, I have difficulty in understanding why anyone can consider not only the special importance I am said to have accorded to the Jews (need I recall who is responsible for this strange 'privileging'?), but the reference I make to the *philosopheme* of the 'death of God' or to Hölderlin's notion of the caesura as belonging to theology or mysticism. I only raise Nietzsche's 'God is dead' here since it figures in a central position in the *Rektoratsrede* and Heidegger refers to it constantly when speaking of nihilism or when he mentions *Unheil* (see chapter 4, note 4) in relation to the Second World War. As for the caesura, which I admit casts a somewhat catastrophic light on history, I am careful to detach the concept from what is, admittedly, its theological support within Hölderlin's thinking. I can very well understand why I am accused of sacrificing the historic to the historial: what I am trying to do is, in fact, to elaborate in the register of the historial an 'event' which Heidegger, for his part, apparently limits himself to classifying as a consequence. I do not know whether I have succeeded in this: it is an attempt, as I fully recognize, which requires a long and difficult labour on historiality and I am only sketching out an outline here. But this outline owes nothing, for good reason, to theology (so far as 'mysticism' is concerned – but what is meant by this exactly? – I reserve my response). If there is a background to my reasoning, then it is to be sought in something like Bataille's emblematization of the execution of Louis XVI. But I should have to come at this in quite other ways, if only because I should have to take into account the Hegelian and Nietzschean philosophies of history or take up again (which does not at all mean accept) what Romantic historiography has dealt with under the heading of the 'symbolic'. My question is this: is it enough merely to invoke

technology (or Capital) to envisage Nazism? Is a philosophical definition of nihilism enough? My – negative – response is perhaps insufficient, but I remain convinced that the question is worth asking.

A second objection, which runs in quite the opposite direction, embarrasses me even more: I argue that there is not the least 'sacrificial' aspect in the *operation* of Auschwitz and, from a place where words are not bandied about lightly, the answer comes back to me: 'yes, there is'.

My intention in denying this sacrificial aspect was initially to exclude religious and, by the same token, theological interpretations, which, all questions of faith apart, I cannot bring myself to see as anything other than, at bottom, self-satisfied and consoling, if not indeed, as I have said, 'self-interested', particularly as they fit in with the psycho-pathological and demonic version of Nazism and, as such, especially in the USA, enter into the process of exculpation of the so-called 'free' world (the American tele-film *Holocaust* is very revealing in this regard – it was this I was thinking of rather than *Shoah* or the poems of Celan). Secondly, it is true that I feel a distinct philosophical reticence about anthropological interpretations of sacrifice, particularly when they are based on the analysis of the scapegoating mechanism and mimetic violence, though I do not deny their explicative power (I have attempted to explain my position on this matter in 'Typographie', in *Mimesis desarticulations* (Paris, Aubier-Flammarion, 1975)). This was as far as my intentions went on this score: I was trying to point out that the massacre had been the work of functionaries. Now, reconsidering the question, I wonder whether in fact, at a quite other level, which would force us at least to re-work the anthropological notion of sacrifice, one should not speak of sacrifice. This is, indeed, an admission that I am purely and simply at a loss – and I remain so. Or, in other words, in this case too, I reserve my response. Or I simply refer the reader to George Steiner's *Language and Silence: Essays on Language, Literature and the Inhuman* (London, Atheneum, 1970).

6

technē

My hypothesis here is that, in all essentials, it is not in the discourse of 1933 that 'Heidegger's politics' is to be found (that discourse, including his *Rectoral Address*, is far too compromised in advance), but in the discourse which follows the 'break' or the 'withdrawal' and which presents itself in any case as a settling of accounts with National Socialism, *in the name of its truth*. As in 1933, but in even more determined fashion, this discourse has at bottom only one theme, *technē*, and this is precisely why it can enlighten us as to the real, or profound, nature of Nazism.

The word *technē* will invariably be translated, throughout these 'dark times' and even beyond them, as *Wissen*, knowledge. With one notable inflection none the less: in 1933, *technē*, associated with *theoria* is connected with *energeia*, itself interpreted as '*Am-Werk-sein*' which we may in effect translate in this context, as Granel does in the French translation, as 'being-at-work' (*être au travail*). Two years later, *energeia* in this sense has disappeared, but the discourse on *technē*, which has in the meantime become a discourse on art, culminates in the definition of art in its essence as '*ins-Werk-setzen*', setting to work, of *alētheia*. 'Work' (*le travail*) has been supplanted by 'the work' (*oeuvre*) and in the very same process, it seems to me, in the innermost 'political' recesses of that discourse, National Socialism has been supplanted by what I shall call a national-aestheticism. There is a vast difference between the two, a difference in which nothing less than the essence of Nazism – and, as a consequence, the essence of politics – is in play.

Let us leave aside the question of work, and therefore, ultimately, of 'socialism'. Granel has said all that needed to be said on this subject[1] and I believe the theme to be a relatively minor and subordinate one in Heidegger's thinking; if not, it would not have fallen out of that thinking so quickly (it was one of the rare philosophical concessions to the programmatic themes of National Socialism, and therefore to the times, which were, as it happened, as much the times of Marx as of Jünger's Nietzsche). The question of art is a much more difficult one to confront. What does Heidegger mean by art?

In the 1945 testament, Heidegger gives a very clear indication of this. He explains first of all what was the deep meaning of his commitment:

> Unimportant as it is in itself, the case of the rectorate 1933–34 would seem to be a sign of the metaphysical state of the essence of science, a science that can no longer be influenced by attempts at its renewal, nor delayed in its essential transformation into pure technology [*Technik*]. This I came to recognize only in the following years (cf. 'The Foundation of the Modern World View through Metaphysics'). The rectorate was an attempt to see in the 'movement' that had come to power, beyond all its failings and crudities, something that reached much farther and that might some day bring about a gathering of what is German unto the historical essence of the West. In no way shall it be denied that at the time I believed in such possibilities and for this reason renounced the thinker's proper vocation in order to help realize them in an official capacity. In no way shall what was caused by my own inadequacy in office be attenuated. But such perspectives don't allow one to see what is essential and moved me to assume the rectorate. The different evaluations of this rectorate that place it against the horizon of academic business as usual may be correct in their way and justified; but they never hit on what is essential. And it is even less possible today to open the horizon of what here is essential to deluded eyes.[2]

In a few words, Heidegger recalls then his two major reasons for joining the Nazi party: the headlong rush of science – i.e. the headlong rush of knowledge or of *techne* in its Graeco-Western definition – towards technicism, which he now believes to be irreversible but which, twelve years before, seemed to him to demand of the University which in his eyes was the guardian of that science, a radical questioning of its essence; and, closely connected with this first reason, the question of the spiritual destination of Germany or, to use the terms employed here, of the 'Western and historial essence of what is German' (François Fédier is right to see the use of the words *das Deutsche* as a quotation from Hölderlin). Heidegger then continues on the subject of 'what is essential', to which attempts to judge his attitude never actually address themselves and the horizon of which it is even more difficult to open up to deluded eyes than it was at the time (at the moment of the upsurge of the 'movement').

> What is essential is that we are caught up in the consummation of nihilism, that God is 'dead', and every time-space for the godhead covered up. The surmounting [*Verwindung*] of nihilism nevertheless announces itself in the poetic thinking and the hymning of what is German [*das Deutsche*]. Of this poetry, however, the Germans still have had the least understanding, because they are concerned to adapt to the measures of the nihilism that surrounds them, and thus to misunderstand the essence of a historial self-affirmation [*Selbstbehauptung*].[3]

Now the idea that the beginnings of 'a *Verwindung*' of nihilism are to be found in poetic thinking and in the hymning of what is German' is something Heidegger never said in 1933. And yet, after his 'withdrawal' this is, in fact, his most constant message. The unqiue motive, so to speak, for this is as follows: There will be no salvation for Germany, i.e. no possibility of the Germans as a people entering (Western/World) history and fulfilling their spiritual-historial destiny, unless they listen to Hölderlin, a man to whom they, as a people in search of itself and seeking to affirm itself as such, have paid not the slightest attention.

What does this statement mean? In extremely schematic terms, we can ascribe the following threefold significance to it:

1 With the failure of the project of *Selbstbehauptung* of the University and, thereby, of Germany itself, science (which supported this whole project)[4] gives way to art, i.e. in this case to 'poetic thought'. This in no way indicates a renunciation of science or thought. But it certainly denotes a re-orientation in the interpretation of the essence of knowledge, of *techne*. Substituting *Denken und Dichten* for science is not without its consequences, at

least in so far as, from this point on, in the project of historial institution or (re)foundation, it is art that is conceived in the first place as harbouring within it the capacity of opening up a possibility of historial *Dasein*. The third of the lectures on 'The Origin of the Work of Art' is perfectly clear on this score. Having said this, however, not for a moment is the schema of historiality that in 1933 justified the summons to self-affirmation called into question. The *Introduction to Metaphysics* (1935) reaffirms forcefully that the only opportunity for foundation lies in the repetition of the grandeur of the Greek beginning, in so far as that grandeur – as grandeur – is still in reserve in the future, that is to say, it is still to come. And this theme, in fact, derives not so much from the Nietzschean conception of history, as *Sein und Zeit* still suggests, but is in fact grounded in the interpretation/translation of the Greeks by Hölderlin: Germany will accede to itself and to History when it is capable of giving resonance to the unsaid and the unthought that is proffered, though still locked away, in the words of the Greeks. For then it will have found its own language.

2   This function may be allotted to art beclause it is in its essence *Dichtung*, and in its turn *Dichtung* is conceived as more essentially *Sprache* (language) and this latter as *Sage*: myth. Only a myth, in other words, is able to allow a people to accede to its own language and thereby to situate itself as such in History. The historial mission of a poet is to bestow his language upon a people. As the *Introduction to Metaphysics* recalls, this was Homer's mission among the Greeks. It could also, for the Germans, be Hölderlin's mission, if they consented to listen to him.

3   'Myth' is to be understood here in the strict sense: Homer's *word* gave Greece its gods. In this 'darkening of the world' and 'time of distress' still aggravated by nihilism, in which no distinction can be made between night and day and where distress is not even felt, in this 'age' stamped with the double negation of the 'no . . . longer' of the Gods that have fled and the 'not . . . yet' of the God to come, the voice of Hölderlin is that prophetic or angelic voice which announces the God who is to come and prepares his coming, or in other words, which 'discovers', by naming, the 'space–time' of the sacred.

Heidegger inherits these themes, in which his philosophy of

History (and consequently his 'politics') are organized, and which he re-works from top to bottom, from a long German tradition which originates in the Jena of Schiller (and not Goethe), the Schlegels, Hölderlin, Schelling and, in part, the 'young Hegel' – and which, through Wagner and Nietzsche, ultimately wins out and certainly at least dominates, in very varying forms, the Germany that did not resist the 'movement' of the 1930s. Leaving aside Heidegger's extreme rigour and the profound level at which he connects with this tradition, what we are dealing with here is no more nor less than a Romanticism, as can be seen very clearly in much weaker 'thinkers' (such as Spengler). It is, moreover, a Romanticism of this kind that structures, both in its caricatural forms (for mass consumption) or its more elaborate (but still degraded) ones, the official – though not always very homogeneous – ideology of the Reich: this is the language of Goebbels and also of Rosenberg, Bäumler or Krieck. In all this discussion of art, there is fierce competition with the *Weltanschauung* (Hitler's favourite concept) of the party and of its master thinkers and Heidegger, however immeasurably different his language and his thought, is always in a dangerous – and clearly perceived – proximity to the language and 'thought' of National Socialism. If only because he wishes to produce its truth.

In two decisive aspects, however, Heideggerian discourse is irreducible to Romanticism:[5]

1 Heidegger accords the utmost seriousness to Hegel's *Aesthetics* – the 'most comprehensive' meditation on art the West possesses, because it is 'conceived on the basis of the whole of metaphysics' – and the verdict it contains concerning the end or death of art. Which means that the question still remains – as *question* – of the possibility of a great art (that is, an art comparable to Greek art), and it remains all the more as a question in that the beginnings of a response can only be found if – and only if – thought will be capable of speaking of art in another language than that of aesthetics which is the language of the whole of philosophy since Plato and Aristotle, i.e. precisely since the end of great art.

2 Heidegger distances himself from the three strategies of the modern which traverse what I shall here call Romanticism, i.e.

two strategies towards the ancient – the dialectical strategy invented by Schiller (the sentimental finds in itself and as itself the opposition of the naive and the sentimental) and the strategy of rebirth represented by Wagner and the early Nietzsche – and a strategy of alleged liberation from the ancient and therefore of self-creation, of which there is a garbled echo in Rosenberg. No modern can in fact be constituted without inventing its relation to the ancient. Indeed the modern consists wholly in such an invention. But whereas the first two strategies call on an antiquity (a Greece), albeit one that is more archaic and authentic, deeper than the one that served as a model for the Renaissance and classicism (this more archaic 'antiquity' is, of course, what will ulimately be called 'dionysiac' in Nietzsche, but it is itself unthinkable without its opposite, that is to say, without its being given form), Heidegger, following Hölderlin's practice directly, 'invents' a Greece which has never actually seen the light of day: repetition in the Heideggerian sense, is repetition of what has not occurred, and that is, moreover, why it is idle to use the term 'strategy' here.[6]

But whatever the differences – and they constitute an unbridgeable gulf between Heidegger and any form of Romanticism, and *a fortiori* National Socialism – Heideggerian discourse on art in its historial (political) project, none the less casts a precise light upon the essence of National Socialism, which has remained more or less veiled in the dominant discourses on the subject.

This is the reason why, I believe, one may venture the term national-aestheticism.

NOTES

1   As has Pierre Rodrigo in his unpublished thesis, 'Le Producteur et le Travailleur (leur portée ontologique chez Marx et Heidegger)', University of Paris I (Panthéon-Sorbonne), 1983.
2   'The Rectorate 1933/4: Facts and Thoughts', pp. 497–8. The lecture referred to, delivered on 9 June 1938, was published in *Holzwege* after the war. An English translation by Majorie Grene entitled 'The Age

of the World-View' appears in *Boundary 2*, vol. 4 (1976); the lecture is also translated as 'The Age of the World Picture' by William Lovitt in *The Question concerning Technology and other essays* (New York, Harper Colophon Books, 1977), pp. 115–54.

3 'The Rectorate 1933/4', p. 498 [translation modified by me to reflect Lacoue-Labarthe's usage, C.T.]. Fédier's French translation of this passage *tones down* Heidegger 's language and deprives it of its vigour and clarity on the essential questions. Heidegger very clearly speaks of the historial self-affirmation of Germany in 1945.

4 The *Rectoral Address* defined science as 'the innermost determining center of all that binds human being to people and state'. The remark referred to the Greeks.

5 In reality, from the philosophical point of view, it is *completely* irreducible to Romanticism. For the simple reason that Romanticism, strictly defined, supposes at its base a metaphysics of the subject. I here term Romanticism, from the perspective of the philosophy of art and history, the tradition which derives, directly or indirectly, from German Idealism.

6 May I be allowed, on this point, to refer to my own essays: 'Hölderlin et les Grecs' and 'L'Antagonisme', in *L'Imitation des modernes* (Paris, Galilée, 1986).

7

The Aestheticization of Politics

Some time around 1935 or 1936, during their period of exile in Denmark, Brecht and Benjamin coined their classic slogan: to the 'aestheticization of politics' one must respond with the 'politicization of art'. In its syntax (overturning), this response is Marxist in type. None the less, it is very strangely consonant with that other watchword, 'politicized science', which the NSDAP students had used not long before against Rector Heidegger. Now it is true that 'politicization' is the starting point of 'totalitarian logic', from which absolutely no one seems to have been immune during this period. However, as regards Nazism, the verdict was incontestably exact: the 'aestheticization of politics' was indeed, in its essence, the programme of National Socialism. Or its project.

In support of this thesis, I shall cite, from among the innumerable documents available, an open letter from Dr Goebbels to Wilhelm Furtwängler, which appeared in the *Lokal-Anzeiger* of 11 April 1933. To Furtwängler who, acknowledging no distinction other than that between 'good' and 'bad' art, had protested against racial discrimination in these matters and the threat this posed to German music, Goebbels replies as follows:

> It is your right to feel as an artist and to look upon matters from the living artistic point of view. But this does not necessarily presuppose your assuming an unpolitical attitude toward the general development that has taken place in Germany. Politics, too, is perhaps an art, if not the highest and most all-embracing there is. Art and artists are not only there to unite; their far more important task is to create a form, to expel the ill trends and make room for the healthy to develop. As a German politician I therefore cannot recognize the

dividing line you hold to be the only one, namely that between good and bad art. Art must not only be good, it must also be conditioned by the exigencies of the people or, rather, only an art that draws on the *Volkstum* as a whole may ultimately be regarded as good and mean something for the people to whom it is directed.[1]

This must not be seen as an isolated declaration. Neither in the writings of Goebbels, for whom this was one of his favourite themes ('Politics is the plastic art of the State'),[2] nor in the work of most of the regime's major ideologues. On the contrary, it is a central theme, as was clearly understood by Hans Jürgen Syberberg whose thinking runs along precisely the lines opened up by Brecht and Benjamin's intuitions. I quote once again, since it is absolutely necessary to do so, taking, first of all, the following passage from *Die freudlose Gesellschaft*, a book written from the greatest depths of German 'distress', after the failure in Germany of the film, *Hitler, a film from Germany*.

The Third Reich as total artwork of a perverted West. We have become accustomed to smiling at the question of 'Hitler and Art' or relegating Nazi architecture, painting, literature or music to the second rank by comparison with the artistic avant-garde. But, as with so many Third Reich phenomena, it is precisely in this matter which it regarded as so significant that one may observe the meeting of tradition and the premonitory signs of the art of the future.

One can also see the artistic will of the Third Reich in quite other places, for example in the layout of its *autobahns*. We have habitually dismissed these *autobahns* which seemed to us products of a socialism that was trying to ingratiate itself by reducing unemployment, as a 'job creation scheme', or else we have relegated them to the rank of sophisticated strategic routes designed for future wars. The problem of unemployment and its·reduction is so important as to deserve our full attention and, if there is one point on which Hitler can hardly be condemned or refuted, it is this one. And besides, military operations have in their time exercized all the ingenuity of a Leonardo da Vinci, to name but one. But leaving these things aside, let us examine and observe how these *autobahns* fit into the landscape: they are the modern roads and arteries of a country which Hitler conceived as a total artwork, comprising a great park lying at the centre of an industrial and peasant society. Seen in this perspective, these *autobahns* radiate out across the landscape of mass industrial society like the pathways running through the gardens of the castles of the feudal era or the municipal parks of the bourgeois age.

Riefenstahl. Hitler understood the significance of film. Now we are just as used to regarding his interest in film pejoratively, as if he had only wished to use it for propaganda purposes. We might even wonder whether he did not merely organize Nuremberg for Leni Riefenstahl, as certain elements might lead us to suppose, and, taking the argument a little further, whether the whole of the Second World War was not indeed conducted as a big budget war film, solely put on so it could be projected as newsreel each evening in his bunker . . . The artistic organization of these mass ceremonies, recorded on celluloid, and even the organization of the final collapse, were part of the overall programme of this movement. Hitler saw the war and its newsreel footage as his heroic epic. The newsreels of the war were the continuation of Riefenstahl's *Triumph of the Will* and her *Nuremberg*. We have often wondered why Hitler, who was continually emphasizing how much he loved Germany, and who was ready to identify with it, destroyed that Germany as he did, why he let it collapse, so quickly going back on his love and his loyalty. But it is precisely in this very identification – Hitler equals Germany – that we find the explanation: it was the horrific and total suicide of Hitler in the form of Germany.

These last lines are obviously an allusion to *Götterdämmerung* in Wagner's *Ring* cycle. Moreover, Syberberg continues immediately:

It is thus that the final victory of Hitler and the Third Reich was not won on the battlefields, but long after the war on the stage of myth, at Bayreuth, via the intermediary of one of his closest disciples, Wieland Wagner.

This does not mean that Syberberg in any sense 'sympathizes with' the Wagnerian aestheticism of National Socialism, even if his relationship with Wagner is a complex one, as can be seen from his *Parsifal* (which is at bottom a – desperate – attempt to snatch Wagner back from national-aestheticism by a simultaneously subtle and violent strategy of re-marking). On the contrary, under the influence of Adorno, he is the first to denounce the degraded, 'kitschy' aesthetics of Nazism.[4] Syberberg's intuition is more profound and, in a sense, it takes the Brechto-Benjaminian verdict literally and radicalizes it. The political model of National Socialism is the *Gesamtkunstwerk* because, as Dr Goebbels very well knew, the *Gesamtkunstwerk* is a political project, since it was the intention of the *Festspiel* of Bayreuth to be for Germany what the Greater Dionysia was for Athens and for Greece as a whole: the place where a people, gathered together in their State, provide themselves with a representation of what they are and what grounds them as such. Which does not merely mean that the work of art (tragedy, music, drama) offers the truth of the *polis* or the State, but that the political itself is instituted and constituted (and regularly re-grounds itself) in and as work of art. That is what the narrator of *Hitler* is, in his own way, saying:

> I believe and avow, I had a dream. The artwork of the state and politics and nation and each individual a part of it, each in his place. The attempt to lead the masses to victory with their inherent strength. In a beautiful race. A model for all others, according to the old pattern two thousand years old and known to every schoolboy from an early age. Like Darwin the Englishman's laws of the struggle for survival, and Wagner's myth from 'Rienzi' to 'Parsifal'. The 'Gesamtkunstwerk' of Germany, the model, I proclaim the death of light, the death of all life and of nature, the end.[5]

The 'old pattern' two thousand years old, which any (German) schoolboy knows, is obviously the Greek pattern and Syberberg refers in quite consciously Platonic terms ('each individual a part of it, each in his place')[6] to the 'artwork of the state'. The total work of art is, in Syberberg's view, cinema. With this conception, he confirms not only the analyses developed by Benjamin in 'The Work of Art in the Age of Mechanical Reproduction',[7] but also Adorno's suspicion of Bayreuth: this vast stage, these characters declaiming against a background of music that is thunderous and uninterrupted – and consequently buried – are in fact the Hollywood aesthetic itself, the 'mass soap opera' with only the technical 'medium' missing (Edison's *camera obscura*, the 'Black Maria', the 'holy apparatus as Mary Pickford said').[8] Already.[9] And Syberberg in fact pushes his diagnosis of the Third Reich as film a long way. Speaking of this latter as 'cultural revolution' ('art for the people. The people's right to self-representation'), though he rejects the Hollywood stereotype of the catastrophe movie, he accepts its inverted form: 'catastrophe as film'.[10] Hitler is 'the greatest film-maker of all time'.

> I, SS man Ellerkamp, Hitler's film projectionist, who knew his most secret desires, his dreams, the things he wanted beyond the real world, two or three movies every day, *Broadway Melody* with Fred Astaire, Walt Disney's *Snow White*, *An Ideal Husband* with Heinz Rühmann, *The Two Seals* with Weiss Ferdl, and almost anything with Weiss Ferdl or Moser or Ruhmann, and Fritz Lang's *Nibelungen* over and over again, *The Hot Punch, Quax the Hard Luck Pilot, The Finances of the Grand Duke*, operettas, *The trouble with Iolanthe*. I saw him greeting Jenny Jugo, Anni Ondra and Leni Riefenstahl. And I saw him joking with Grett Szlezak, Renata Müller, Olga Tchechowa, Paula Wessely, and Lili Dagover.
>
> I saw him watching the French movies he banned for the public. I saw Goebbels keeping Chaplin's films away from him, but he did hand over *Gone with the Wind*.
>
> Yes, the man who controls the cinema controls the future. There is only one future, the future of the cinema, and he knew that, the man whom they called 'Gröfaz', the 'greatest general of all time'. Some used the nickname reverently, others with nasty irony. But I know he was really the greatest, the greatest film-maker of all time.[11]

This critique chimes in with the 1960s situationist critique, from a Marxist perspective, of the consumerist 'society of the spectacle'. For example, Syberberg has the puppet of Ludwig II of Bavaria say: 'I warned you. I, Ludwig II, I warned you from the very outset, I warned that business, wheeling and dealing, movies, porno, politics, were a show for the masses. Entertainment, let money roll in, it has to ...'[12]. Yet the Situationists, however radical their analyses, remained caught up in a sort of Rousseauist reverie of *appropriation* – which was in the end merely set against all forms of *representation* (from the image to the delegation of power). There is no naiveté of this kind in Syberberg, but a strict idea of technical irreversibility. Naiveté is no doubt the price one pays for passionate revolutionary enthusiasm and it was undeniably necessary in the unmasking of the spectacular as such.[13] But the logic of *technē* is – always – more convoluted than the simple system of oppositions in which one – always – claims to confine it; it might even be said that it is this which unravels every system of oppositions, and this is what Syberberg cannot be unaware of from his art, which is also a technique.

But behind this critique of the tendency for the world – and the sphere of politics – to turn into cinema, and behind the emphatic declarations of Goebbels and certain others, as Syberberg is also aware, there lies a whole tradition which in fact goes back two thousand years, or at least the dream this tradition has engendered in German thought since the end of the *Aufklärung*. And this dream is, in fact, a dream of the City as work of art.

We should, of course, differentiate within German thought. Schlegel certainly does not dream in the same way as Hölderlin or Hegel; who, in turn, do not dream like Nietzsche for example. None the less there are common features which are very easily identifiable (probably because all these hugely diverse 'dreams' have their origins in a single 'diurnal residue': their reading of Winckelmann). Of these features, I should like here to discuss three which seem crucial:

(1) The political (the City) belongs to a form of *plastic art, formation and information, fiction* in the strict sense. This is a deep theme which derives from Plato's politico-pedagogic writings (especially *The Republic*) and reappears in the guise of such concepts as *Gestaltung* (configuration, fashioning) or *Bildung*, a term with a revealingly polysemic character (formation, constitution, organization, education, culture etc.). The fact that the political is a form of plastic art in no way means that the *polis* is an artificial or conventional formation, but that the political belongs to the sphere of *technē* in the highest sense of the term, that is to say in the sense in which *technē* is conceived as the accomplishment and revelation of *physis* itself. This is why the *polis* is also 'natural': it is the 'beautiful formation' that has spontaneously sprung from the 'genius of a people' (the Greek genius) according to the modern – but in fact very ancient – interpretation of Aristotelian mimetology.[14]

(2)   The Greeks are the people of art and, by that token, the
political people *par excellence*. It fell to Hegel, in his *Lectures on the
Philosophy of History*,[15] to provide what one might call the
definitive version of this proposition. In its fundamental determination, he explains, the Greek genius is such that 'the freedom
of the spirit is conditioned [*bedingt*] and is essentially related to an
impulse of nature' [*Naturerregung*]: 'the activity of the spirit does
not yet possess here in itself the matter and organ for expression,
but it has need of the stimulus and matter of nature: it is not yet
free spirituality determining itself, but naturalness formed into
spirituality'. This is why 'the Greek genius is the plastic artist who
forms the stone into a work of art'.

In other words, this comes down to saying that Greece is quite
simply the very home of *technē* (or – and this makes no difference
– of *mimēsis*). Ultimately this will have been what Hegel was
always saying – and what Germany was always thinking with
him. Now the three manifestations of the Greek genuis thus
defined, in Hegel's systematic presentation of them, culminate in
what Hegel calls 'the political work of art': the subjective work of
art is, in effect 'the formation (Bildung) of man himself', the
'beautiful corporeality' fashioned for example by sport in which
the body transforms itself into an 'organ of the spirit' (this theme,
taken from Winckelmann and passed on through Hölderlin's
thoughts on the 'athletic virtue' of the Greeks will run through
German history right down to the 1936 Olympics and the policy
of the Third Reich on sport). The objective work of art, on the
other hand, is the 'form of the divine world', art as religion (or
vice versa) whose object is 'the very concept of the Greek spirit',
that is to say, the transformation of the divine as 'natural power'
into the divine as 'spiritual power' (this analysis is based, as we
know, on the interpretation of tragedy as a site of conflict between
old and new gods, or as the site of a division of ethical substance:
beyond the strictly Hegelian thematization of this conflict, this
again is a constant motif in the German tradition from Hölderlin –
or even indeed from Schiller – through to Heidegger, the theme of
the two Greeces). Finally, the State 'unites the two . . . sides of the
subjective and objective work of art. In the State, the spirit is not

only the object formed as divine, not only shaped [*ausgebildet*] subjectively into beautiful corporeality, but is a living, general [*allgemein*] spirit which is also the self-conscious spirit of particular individuals.'

Here again, the particular determinations Hegel's thought imprints upon this intutition are of little import. Nietzsche, for example, had a very similar intuition in the years when he was writing the *Birth of Tragedy*.[16] Unlike Hegel, however, he accorded only very limited attention to democracy and law. None the less, when dealing with the Greeks, both men identified politics with aesthetics and such an identification is at the heart of the mimetic *agon* in which they both (and many others with them – in fact, almost everyone, including Heidegger) saw Germany's only chance of finding its identity and acceding to existence.[17]

One might even say that Hegel truly hit the mark when he spoke of a religion of art. He meant the term 'religion' in the broadest sense, that is to say the sense in which *religare* (though this is a Latin word, and a Latin model)[18] includes the political. This is the sense in which Wagner will understand it. And this is also how Heidegger , who had a great many reasons to be wary of Wagner, would credit him, none the less, with having sought to restore the possibility – in spite of the Hegelian verdict on the 'death' of art – of something like a 'great art': 'With reference to the historical position of art, the effort to produce the 'collective artwork', remains essential. The very name is demonstrative. For one thing, it means that the arts should no longer be realized apart from one another, that they should be conjoined in *one* work. But beyond such sheer quantitative unification, the artwork should be a celebration of the national community, it should be *the* religion.[19]

(3)   In its essence the political is *organic*. We must allow the term to resonate doubly here and hear the *ergon* that lies beneath the *organon*. This is where the truth of what is called 'totalitarianism' is concealed.

To say that the political is organic does not simply mean that the State is conceived simultaneously as 'living totality' and as artwork. The State is still too abstract a notion, which is to say that it is still too separate a reality (and on this point, if one leaves out of account Hegel's last writings, almost the whole of the German tradition is agreed, including Marx and Nietzsche). The essential organicity of the political is in reality infra-political, if not indeed infra-social (in the sense of *Gesellschaft*). It is the organicity of the community: the *Gemeinschaft* or as Heidegger says in his commentary upon the *Republic*, the *Gemeinwesen*. Consequently, it is the organicity of the people, the *Volkstum*, which our concept of 'nation', restored to its original meaning, renders reasonably well, in so far as it indicates a natural or 'physical' determination of the community which can only be accomplished and revealed to that community by a technē – if not indeed by *technē* itself, by art, beginning with language (with the community's language). If *technē* can be defined as the sur-plus of *physis*, through which *physis* 'deciphers' and presents itself – and if, therefore, *technē* can be said to be *apophantic* in the Aristotelo-Heideggerian sense of the term[20] – political *organicity* is the *surplus* necessary for a nation to present and recognize itself. And such is the political function of art.

It goes without saying that there is nothing – except a misinterpretation of the essence of *physis* – compelling this political logic to come to be grounded in a biologism and to substitute the race for the nation (or the language community). But it can very easily be taken in that direction once *physis* comes to be interpreted as *bios* on the authority of a 'science'. This is, however, merely a consequence of the *organic* interpretation of the political. Racism – and anti-semitism in particular – is primarily, fundamentally, an aestheticism. (In his essence, 'the Jew' is a caricature: ugliness itself.) This is why racism goes hand in hand, no less fundamentally, with a massive unleashing of *technē*, which is in fact its radical transmutation into *excrescence*, which proceeds increasingly to conceal *physis*, whose limits it oversteps, having lost sight of or 'forgotten' them.[21] There is a kind of 'lethal' essence of technology, which means that its 'everything is possible' does in fact end up introducing, that is to say *bringing about*, if not the impossible, then at least the unthinkable (Extermination or genetic manipulation – and the latter is still on the agenda today).

The *organic* conception of the political finds its definition in what Jean-Luc Nancy has suggested we call 'immanentism' to replace what is in fact the very vague term 'totalitarianism', even though the themes of *totale Mobilmachung* (Jünger), the *totale Staat* (Carl Schmitt) or, in Italy, the *Stato totalitario* (identified with the *Impero romano*) mean that it is not entirely obsolete.[22] As, of course, does the work of Hannah Arendt. By 'immanentism', Nancy means a condition in which it is 'the aim of the community of beings in essence to produce their own essence as their work (*oeuvre*), and moreover to produce precisely this essence *as community*'.[23] In other words, in immanentism it is the community itself, the people or the nation, that is the work (*oeuvre*) following the conception acknowledged by Romanticism of the work as subject and the subject as work: the 'living artwork' indeed, though this in no way prevents it from working lethally.[25] The infinitization or absolutization of the subject, which is at the heart of the metaphysics of the Moderns, here finds its strictly operational outcome: the community creating, the community at work creates and works itself, so to speak, thereby accomplishing the subjective process *par excellence*, the process of self-formation and self-production. This is why that process finds its truth in 'a fusion of the community' (in festival or war) or in the ecstatic identification with a Leader who in no way represents any form of transcendence, but incarnates, in immanent fashion, the immanentism of a community. And this is also why a will to immediate effectuation or self-effectuation underlies national-aestheticism. This will to immediacy is precisely what has been caesura-ed, for it was, ultimately, the crime – the boundless excess – of Nazism.

NOTES

1 Quoted in Viktor Reimann, *The Man who created Hitler* (London, William Kimber, 1977), p. 171.
2 This phrase is from a novel Goebbels wrote in his youth. It is quoted by Paul de Man in 'Hegel on the Sublime', *Displacement=Derrida and After* (Indiana University Press, 1983).
3 Syberberg, *Die freudlose Gesellschaft: Notizen aus dem letzten Jahr* (Munich/Vienna, Hanser, 1981), pp. 74–5.

4   In one of the last sequences of the *Hitler* film, the protean narrator Koberwitz addresses Hitler in the following terms, accusing him of being responsible, at all levels, for the definitive non-existence of Germany:

> You took away our sunsets, sunsets by Caspar David Friedrich. You are to blame that we can no longer look at a field of grain without thinking of you. You made old Germany kitschy with your simplifying words and peasant pictures ... The wretched artist as a hangman degenerating into a politician, voluntarily cheered as no man ever before. How can I make this clear to you and to me, and me and all the children and grandchildren who didn't know all this, this previous life which they have all forgotten by now, corrupted by the new legacy of your time. The new old philistine ... All this, all this has been made impossible. The words 'magic' and 'myth' and 'serving' and 'ruling', 'führer', 'authority', are ruined, are gone, exiled to eternal time. And we are snuffed out. Nothing more will grow here. An entire nation stopped existing, in the diaspora of the mind and the elite ... (*Hitler: a film from Germany* (Manchester, Carcanet, p. 242))

5   *Hitler: a film from Germany*, p. 234.
6   Need we recall here the reply of the Athenian in *The Laws* to the tragic poets who are requesting entry to the city he is defining: 'Most excellent of Strangers, we ourselves to the best of our ability, are the authors of a tragedy at once superlatively fair and good; at least, all our polity is framed as a representation of the fairest and best life, which is in reality, as we assert, the truest tragedy. Thus we are composers of the same things as yourselves, rivals of yours as artists and actors of the fairest drama, which, as our hope is, true law, and it alone, is by nature competent to complete' (Plato, *Laws*, Bk VII (London, Heinemann, 1968), p. 99. This very old scene, if not indeed archi-scene, of mimetic rivalry between the poet and the politician is replayed in Syberberg's *Hitler*. To the narrator Koberwitz, who accuses him of having destroyed German cinema, the Hitler puppet replies: 'Ha, just look at you. Like Murnau, Lubitsch, Sternberg. Like Fritz Lang. They accepted you, back then, at the academy in Vienna. You could have become an artist. And I, I had to produce my world in politics. You did not sacrifice yourself to do the dirty business of politics. I didn't goldbrick, and I did my job to

the best of my abilities, our old tradition …' (ibid., p. 202) But obviously the tone is no longer the same.

7 W. Benjamin, *Illuminations*, trans. Harry Zohn (London, Fontana, 1973), pp. 219–44.

8 *Hitler: a film from Germany*, p. 246.

9 Adorno, *Versuch über Wagner*, (Munich/Zurich, 1964).

10 *Hitler, a film from Germany*. This section not translated in the English edition cited above.

11 Ibid., p. 109.

12 Ibid, p. 44.

13 Guy Debord, *The Society of the Spectacle* (Detroit, Black and Red, 1973).

14 I shall come back to this point. The interpretation of *mimesis* as genius, as natural gift by which *physis* is completed, reaches its high point in Kant's third *Critique*, but it is, from Longinus onwards, one of the dominant themes in thinking on the sublime (I have attempted to demonstrate this in 'La Vérité sublime', *Po&sie* 38 (1986). This is how the idea of the political 'beautiful formation' can fit in with the famous opening of Aristotle's *Politics* in which the city in general is said to exist 'by nature' (Bk I, 2, 1252b 30). Moreover, the justification Aristotle gives of it, by its appeal to a final cause, runs in precisely this direction: 'Because it is the completion of associations existing by nature, every polis exists by nature, having itself the same quality as the earlier associations from which it grew. It is the end or consummation to which those associations move, and the 'nature' of things consists in their end or consummation (physis is here to be understood in the sense of form) … Again … the end or final cause is the best. Now self-sufficiency is the end, and so the best; (and on this it follows that the state brings about the best, and is therefore natural, since nature always aims at bringing about the best)' (*The Politics of Aristotle*, ed. and trans. by Ernest Barker (London, OUP, 1958), p. 5). If we also take into account that this 'naturalness' of the city allows man to be defined as a *zoon politikon* and that he is only such because he is a *zoon logon echon* (1253a), it is only a small step to arrive at chapter 4 of the *Poetics* in which man is defined as the *zoon mimetikotaton* (48b).

15 Hegel, *Vorlesungen über die Philosophie der Geschichte* (Stuttgart, Reclam, 1961), pp. 339–54.

16 See, especially, Nietzsche, 'Nachgelassene Fragmente, Ende 1870 – April 1871', *Werke*, section III, vol. 3, pp. 145–225.

17 This is at least true of the young Hegel, the one who deplored that 'the state of man, whom the times have driven back into an inner world, can be nothing other, when he wishes to stay alive, than an eternal death . . . His pain co-exists with an awareness of the limits which make him scorn life such as it is permitted to him.' Kostas Papaioannou, basing his analysis upon Hegel's writings before 1806, describes this movement most accurately : 'the happiness that emanates from the "beautiful Greek totality" is the opposite of the German misery, which condemns the finest minds to seek refuge "in an inner world" tormented by despair and "death". The political idealization of Greece serves principally as grounds for a triple attack on the 'political hopelessness' of Germany, the apoliticism of the bourgeois world and Christian escapism. Germany 'has never been a nation' . . . Germany 'is not a State' . . . Whilst France is 'embarked upon a vast political experiment' . . . the Germans show that they are incapable of defending themselves and aspire only to protect their private property: beyond that, 'the power of the State seems to them something alien that exists outside of them' . . . By contrast, 'the citizen of the ancient world lived as a free man obeying laws he had made for himself. He sacrificed his property, his passions and his life for a reality that was his own' . . . he *strove* for an 'idea' and 'before that idea his individuality disappeared' (*Hegel* (Paris, Seghers, 1959), pp. 26–7). I do not suppose it is necessary to remind the reader how much Marx would concur with this *protest* – and indeed share its rationale.

18 This ambiguity would never be eliminated: in the mimetic *agon* it entered into with the Ancient world, Germany sought, in the will that it displayed from the *Sturm und Drang* period onwards to dissociate itself from a 'Latin' style *imitatio* (of Italian and, most especially, of French type: the political stakes involved in this are immense), another Greece than that late one which had been transmitted to modern Europe through the Roman filter. Ultimately, if Germany exists, it is as a force of resistance against Rome and all its various substitutes (France from Louis XIV to the two Napoleonic Empires and even beyond; Czarism, which is to say oriental Caesarism, either in its traditional or its 'socialist' form). This can be seen in the fracture produced by the Lutheran Reformation: It is no accident that this coincides in its geographical extension with the imperial *limes*. Germany only invents what I shall call the double Greece, that is to say a Greece which is tragic and torn, on the lines of the very division – which is, above all, a sacred one – within Athenian tragedy (*orchestra/skene*), in order to reach a model that is

more *archaic* in the fullest sense of the term. That is why Germany, having discovered the oriental (mystical, enthusiastic, nocturnal, savage – *natural*) depths of Greece, regularly identified itself with what one might, from an historico-political point of view, term its 'Doric order' (Hölderlin's 'Junonian', Nietzsche's 'Apollinian': rigorous, circumscribed, solar – *technical*). And it is obviously here that Rome, which received only that heritage – though shorn of its hellenistic mawkishness and restored to its austere military, peasant and civic grandeur – becomes superimposed on the image, which was presented as intact, of Greece. The inaugural gesture of National Socialism is no less Roman, for this reason, nor Sparto-Roman, than the founding gestures of the French Revolution, the Consulate or the Napoleonic Empire. There was something of Petronius in Wagner, something of Nero in Hitler. Syberberg has meditated upon a planetary *'Qualis artifex pereo'*.

19 *Nietzsche*, vol. 1, pp. 85–6.

20 *Being and Time* (Oxford, Basil Blackwell, 1962), para. 7. I shall come back to this point.

21 It is in this sense that Heidegger, in the last paragraphs of 'Overcoming Metaphysics', having evoked the 'desolated earth which is only supposed to be of use for the guarantee of the dominance of man' and the whole of human activity reduced to judging whether something is important or unimportant for 'life', i.e. the 'will to will', can write this: 'The unnoticeable law of the earth preserves the earth in the sufficiency of the emerging and perishing of all things in the allotted sphere of the possible which everything follows, and yet nothing knows. The birch tree never oversteps its possibility. The colony of bees dwells in its possibility. It is first the will which arranges itself everywhere in technology that devours the earth in the exhaustion and consumption and change of what is artificial. Technology drives the earth beyond the developed sphere of its possibility into such things which are no longer a possibility and are thus the impossible' (*The End of Philosophy*, trans, Joan Stambaugh (London, Souvenir, 1973), p. 109. This obviously echoes the chorus in the second *stasimon* of *Antigone* (*Polla ta deina* …) which Heidegger commented upon at least twice in the Nazi years (cf. *The Introduction of Metaphysics* and 'Hölderlins Hymne "Der Ister"' (1942), *Gesamtausgabe*, (Klostermann, Frankfurt-am-Main, 1984), vol. 53. The *Introduction to Metaphysics* ends with these lines of Hölderlin's:' For the mindful God abhors untimely growth' (*Aus dem Motivkreis der Titanen*).

22 Cf. 'Le soldat du travail', *Recherches*, 32–3 (September 1978)

23 Jean-Luc Nancy, *La Communauté désoeuvrée* (Paris, Christian Bourgois Editeur, 1986).
24 Cf. P. Lacoue-Labarthe, J.-L. Nancy, *L'Absolu littéraire* (Paris, Le
Seuil, 1978).
25 'The political or collective undertakings which are dominated by a
will to absolute immanence, have as their truth the truth of death.
Immanence, communial fusion contains no other logic than that of
the suicide of the community which orders itself according to that
immanence. Thus the logic of Nazi Germany was not only a logic of
exterminating the other – the sub-human outside the communion of
blood and soil – but also, virtually, a logic of sacrifice of all those
within the 'Aryan' community, who did not satisfy the criteria of
pure immanence, with the result that a plausible extrapolation of the
process could have been represented by the suicide of the German
nation itself: moreover, it would not be wrong to say that did in fact
take place, so far as certain respects of the spiritual reality of the
nation were concerned' (*la Communauté désoeuvrée*, pp. 35–6). I am
not sure that I entirely agree, however: the logic of 'immanentism' –
which is very formidable – certainly includes murder, which is to
say, first of all, that it includes sacrifice. But it is also a logic of the
'will to live', and indeed of the 'will to survive' (the Thousand Year
Reich). It is undeniable that there is a sort of suicidal act in
unleashing war, but it is precisely this unleashing which precipitates
the Extermination. The process of immanentist infinitization passes,
in fact, through death, if death is conceived as 'the infinite accomplishment of an immanent life' (ibid., p. 37). The Extermination
does not, however, correspond to this logic. Nor to that of the
exclusion of the other. And this is why it is more serious: not so
much on account of the will purely and simply to annihilate but on
account of the very people to whom that will to annihilate applies,
the Jews, in so far as they are reckoned neither to belong to the
community nor to stand outside it, that is to say in so far as they are
literally unlocatable or – and this comes down to the same thing –
forbidden to exist from the outset. This topological monstrosity has
its origins in a quite other logic than that of immanence; it originates
in fact in a mimetology, which means, that the frenzied or delirious
immanentism of the *organic* community is itself governed by a
double bind which divides or 'schizes' the intimacy of the community,
as soon as its project is formulated. I shall return to this point later.
    Moreover, in the logic I am trying to reconstitute here, I would
happily speak of a violent *abortion* of Germany in its frenzied attempt

to appropriate itself as such (to identify itself) and to step into the light of history. Germany would be a nation which had never been granted *birth*, the pure contradiction of a stillborn political subject, condemned to lead a ghostly 'existence' in the outer reaches.

8

The Truth of the Political

Unlike despotism of the Stalinist type, and therefore unlike Soviet-style 'totalitarianism', National Socialism remains very largely resistant to the methods of political and ideological analysis. Basically, it continues to be quite simply 'inexplicable' and, by that token, never ceases to haunt modern consciousness as a sort of endlessly latent 'potentiality', both stored away and yet constantly at hand within our societies. The fact is that National Socialism at no point presented itself as a determinate politics – even if it did have a clearly determinate *ideology*, as has been brilliantly demonstrated by Hannah Arendt – but rather as the *truth* of the political. In that respect, it both exposed to the light of day and just as quickly obscured the non-political essence of the political which no 'politology', nor even any political philosophy, is able to define. But if this essence of the political is to be sought in art, no aesthetic, nor any philosophy of art either, is capable of undoing the unseverable link between art and politics, because its categories, practically all of which have their origins in Platonism, have at their roots the presupposition, dominant throughout the whole philosophical tradition, that the political ('religion') is the truth of art. This is why Heidegger, in so far as his project in the 1930s explicitly consists in 'overcoming' aesthetics,[1] gives a privileged access – and perhaps the only possible access – to the essence of the political that is simultaneously veiled and unveiled by National Socialism. It is also necessary to read Heidegger on this point in what he does not manage to say or, more strictly, in what is ceaselessly slipping away – though never failing to leave its trace and its mark – in what he is seeking to say. This is so for two reasons. The first is Heidegger's involvement, in spite of the 'break' of 1934, with National Socialism – on the basis, essentially, of a kind of 'transcendental illusion' bearing on the people and restoring a subject (of history) at a point where the thinking of ek-static *Dasein* and finitude (of temporality as 'original outside-itself' (*hors-de-soi originaire*)) should have prevented any confusion of *Mitsein* with a notion of community as substance (*substance communielle*) or even, quite simply, with an entity (the people, whether Greek or German, which is to say, their language). The other reason, which is much more difficult to grasp, is the fact of Heidegger submitting most enigmatically to the philosophical (in this case Platonic) condemnation of *mimesis* (invariably seen as involving the determination of truth as *homoiôsis* and *adaequatio*);[2] whereas the thinking of *technē* derives in rigorously Aristotelian fashion, from a fundamental mimetology.[3]

In these circumstances, what is the partial insight Heidegger offers?

First of all, one sees rather clearly, that National Socialism fits into that agonal history of Germany, the best known thematization of which is that found in the second of Nietzsche's *Untimely Meditations*. When in 1933 he called upon Germany to re-commence the Greek beginning, Heidegger was basing himself upon such an agonistic interpretation of history (in *Sein und Zeit* he had in fact explicitly related this to Nietzsche). It is not because he himself places himself within such a historiographical tradition and might therefore be projecting illusorily on to National Socialism his own concept of history; but it is because he very clearly sees the 'movement' as proceeding from such a history, and doing so moreover quite consciously, in other words with the aim of accomplishing that history. The agonistic (and consequently mimetic) rivalry with the Ancient World obviously does not only apply to Germany alone. It is one of the general foundations of the modern political sphere, being quite simply the invention of the Modern itself, i.e., of what appears in the era of the de-legitimation of Christian theocracies. Since the Renaissance, Europe as a whole has been prey to the Ancient and it is *imitatio* which governs the construction of the Modern. What distinguishes Germany, however, is the fact that, from the Revolution onwards, or rather from its imperialistic accomplishment, which coincides with the appearance of speculative idealism, or, as Granel has it, with 'the Reformation's entry on to the scene of philosophy', Germany rejected the neo-classical – and Latin – style of that *imitatio* (which also implies the rejection of the political form in which neo-classicism ultimately clothed itself, i.e. the Republican form) and sought, not without difficulty, to find a style of its own.[4] But the task was, as we know, virtually – if not indeed – totally impossible. For one thing, the German *imitatio*, essentially induced by the French one, is already a second-order phenomenon, which made its difficulties even more pronounced: a mimetic *agon* with France was thus added to that with Greece, such that it was not merely a question of wresting from France the monopoly over ancient models (and therefore over art, culture and civilization), but it became necessary also to 'invent' a Greece which had up to that point remained unimitated, a sort of meta-Greece if you will, which would allegedly be at the foundation of Greece itself (but which then also ran the risk of never really having taken place in itself). The discovery of 'enthusiastic' Greece, i.e. the discovery of the 'authentic' religion of the Greeks and the re-evaluation of their myths, was the means employed in this invention, which ultimately pre-supposed that Christianity be considered an imported (Eastern) religion, foreign to the 'European spirit'[5] and Rome viewed as the first model of bad *imitatio*. At a deeper level, in reality, the constraint governing *imitatio*, the mimetological law, demands that *imitatio* rid itself of *imitatio* itself, or that, in what it establishes (or has imposed upon it) as a model, it should address something that does not derive from *imitatio*. What the German *imitatio* is seeking in Greece is the model – and therefore the possibility – of a pure emergence, of a pure originality: a model of self-formation.[6] And this also explains the implacable contradiction that inhabits the *imitatio* when radicalized to this point. Whether or not it be induced by the model (though we should bear in mind autochthony, and accept that German Greece cannot be reduced to a pure projection), the demand for the *imitatio* of a self-formation, which is, according to Kant, the very demand that must be met for there to be any heritage or transmission of a people's genius, produces a pure double bind. All in all, Germany, in its attempt to accede to historical existence and to be, as people or nation, 'distinguishable in the world's history'[7] quite simply aspired to genius. But genius is by definition inimitable. And it is therefore in the impossibility of this imitation of genius that Germany literally exhausted itself, succumbing to a sort of psychosis or historico-spiritual schizophrenia, of which certain of its most highly regarded geniuses, from Hölderlin to Nietzsche, were the heralds (and premonitory victims). And besides, only a schizophrenic logic was capable of allowing that unthinkable event, the Extermination; and the present division of Germany is virtually a symbolic outcome of that process. Germany still does not exist. Except in the distress of not existing.[8]

As for the political sphere – at least the modern political sphere – this fate reveals that for Germany the crucial process was – and probably still is – that of national identification. Nietzsche felt this intuitively – and the point was not in itself 'nationalistic'. He, with his distrust of socialism and America, did not believe that it was work or production, nor even man's self-production, that were decisive in the political or historical spheres, but the self-formation of peoples according to their capacity for art. The term 'identification' is, however, borrowed from Freud,[9] because it is ultimately the only one we possess to designate what is at stake in the mimetic process and, above all, because once eased out of its aesthetico-psychological context, in which it in fact remains problematical,[10] it can be drawn into the stronger network of the proper (or 'own': *le propre*) and appropriating, of appropriation and de-propriation or disappropriation etc. Oversimplifying to excess, it can be said that, at least since Plato, education or training, political *Bildung*, has been thought taking the mimetic process *as starting point*: Plato challenges this, dreaming precisely of a (philosophical) self-grounding of the political, i.e. cutting through the mimetological double bind – admittedly with an idea of the Idea that is itself paradigmatic (and belonging, in consequence, to the mimetological). Conversely in the sphere of the accomplishment of the philosophical – and, which is indissociable from it from the outset, of the overturning of Platonism – the programme emerges of what Schiller calls an 'aesthetic education' of humanity. The inversion of 'values' matters little to us here. The crucial point is that *Bildung* is always thought on the basis of archaic mythic *paideia*, which is to say that it is thought on the basis of what the Romans were to understand as *exemplarity*. It is not by chance that the 'myth' of the Cave – a myth that has no 'mythic' source, a myth that is self-formed and self-grounded – lays the foundations of Plato's political project. Identification or appropriation – the self-becoming of the Self – will always have been thought as the appropriation of a model, i.e. as the appropriation of a means of appropriation, if the model (the example) is the ever paradoxical imperative of propriation: imitate me in order to be what you are. One can see without difficulty from the empirical–anthropological description of this process exactly how it works and René Girard, basing himself in actual fact upon Kojève's interpretation of the dialectics of desire in Hegel's *Phenomenology* , has given an excellent account of it (but is not the dialectic precisely the maintenance of the hope that the double bind can be resolved or, in other words, that the paradoxicality of mimesis can be overcome?).[11] Yet the question still remains of how, and above all why, identity (properness/property (*la propriété*) or being-in-oneself/ being-proper (*être-propre*)) derives from mimetic appropriation.

It is by no means obvious that self-identity presupposes that there be an other, because, to put it quite simply, the other also presupposes the identical. The Hegelian formulation of the dialectical principle, according to which identity is the identity of identity and difference in fact presupposes an original attribution of identity. The speculative dialectic is an eschatology of the identical; and so long as this logic, more or less explicitly, underpins the interpretation of *mimesis*, one can only ever move endlessly from the same to the other – under the authority of the same. Conceived more rigorously, however, mimetologic (*la mimétologique*) complicates and de-stabilizes this schema: in the dialecticization of mimetism, a subject is presupposed, albeit a virtual one. But, by definition, mimetism forbids such a presupposition, and this has been very convincingly established by Diderot: no subject, potentially identical to himself or related to himself, can pre-exist the mimetic process, except to render it impossible. If something pre-exists, it is not even, as Plato believed, a substance, in the form of a pure malleability or plasticity which the model would come to stamp as its own 'type' or on which it would imprint its image. Such a substance is, in reality, already a subject, and it is not on the basis of an eidetics that one can hope to think the mimetic process, if the *eidos* – or, more generally, the figural – is the very presupposition of the identical. And it is, moreover, because from Plato to Nietzsche and Wagner and through to Jünger – and even to Heidegger who, at least as the reader of Trakl, actually taught us this[12] – such an eidetics underpins mimetology in the form of what I have felt might be called an onto-typology, that an entire tradition (the one that culminates in Nazism) will have thought that the political is the sphere of the *fictioning* of beings and communities.

If the slightest hope remains of having done with 'political fiction' – and I am not sure that it does – then we should have to make of *mimesis* something other than the *virtus dormitiva* of social anthropology and the 'miraculous' explanation of association and dissociation. We have therefore to try to think it in its possibility.

Under what conditions is *imitatio* possible? There are at least two:

1   The subject of the imitation (subjective genitive) or, in other words, the imitant, has to be nothing in and of itself or must, in Diderot's words have 'nothing characteristic of itself'. It therefore must not already be a subject. This supposes an inherent im-propriety (*impropriété*), an 'aptitude for all roles' – on condition, however, that this im-propriety or this aptitude should not in turn be considered as subject or support. (This could be the 'negative' variant – negative as in negative theology – of onto-typology.)

2   The 'subject of the imitation' therefore must be a 'being' (in the sense of being something which is, an essent) originally *open to (ouvert à)* or originally 'outside itself', ek-static. This is precisely what Heideggerian *Da-sein* 'is'. But this ecstatic (de)constitution has itself to be thought as lack or as insufficiency – according to a strict thinking of finitude. The subject is originally the infirmity of the subject and this infirmity is its very intimacy, in a state of dehiscence. Or, in other words, differance is inherent in the subject, forever preventing it from being *subject* (or, in other words, from being a *stable* essent) and essentially determining it as mortal. Jacques Derrida has suggested that I should give the name

desistance to this inherent infirmity, without which no relation (either to oneself or to others) could be established and there would be neither consciousness nor sociality.[13]

The 'subject' desists. This is why it is fictionable at its very origin and only accedes to selfhood, if it ever does, through being supplemented by a model or models which precede it. It is always possible to give a dialectical description of this process since it ultimately depends upon an originary mediation. But one can only do so by creating a teleology of self-identity which comes back down to designating desistance as a *moment*, even if it be the first moment. Now the whole problem is probably that desistance resists. In other words, it remains paradoxically constitutive and it is this that Lacan has pointed out in speaking of 'pre-inscription in language', even if the theme of 'prematuration', the mirror phase or the description of the 'individual myth of the neurotic'[14] give rise to a dialecticizing schema (Lacan does not use the term 'dialectic of desire' lightly). In reality, we have to wrest mimetism away from the classical conceptions of *imitatio* and rethink it in the light of a rigorous mimetology.

The structure of original supplementarity is the very structure of the relation between *technē* and *physis*. In Philostratus's *Imagines*, we find this strange proposition:

... Βασανιζοντι δε την γενεσιν της τεχνης μιμησις μεν ευρημα πρεσβυτατον χαι ξυγγενεστατον τη φυσει

... but, seriously to return to the origin of art, imitation is one of the earliest inventions, as old as nature itself.[15]

Between *physis* and *technē*, the relation is therefore one of congeniality: *technē* and *physis* share the same origin. How are we to understand this if not in terms of what Heidegger constantly offers to be thought, namely that *technē* is the deputizing function (*la suppléance*) demanded by the essential 'cryptophilia' of *physis* or, which comes down to the same thing, of the *lethe* that is constitutive of *alētheia*? This is why *technē [mimesis]* is not representation in the sense of a second, specular presentation or a reproductive, duplicative one, but representation in the full sense of the word, i.e. in the sense of *making present*. The difficult thing is, as ever, to think an originary secondarity – or rather to think the origin as second, as initially divided and deferred, which is to say in differance (*en différance*). In other words, the difficulty is to think the *En diaphero heautô*, the Same, without submitting it to the logic of identity. But it was precisely Heraclitus's formula which, for Hölderlin, designated the essence of the beautiful (of art). It was from this starting point that he thought through the paradoxicality of mimesis,[16] the logic of which – or what I have called, for want of a better term, its hyperbologic (which is a logic of inifinite alternation and 'harmonic' tension) – in spite of all appearances, thwarts dialectical logic and, so to speak, destabilizes it in advance. This is the case from the essays of the Homburg period onwards:

> In pure life, Nature and Art are only harmonically opposed to each other. Art is the bloom, the fulfilment of nature. Nature only becomes divine through its link with art, which is different but harmonic, when each of the two is entirely what it can be and each is bound to the other, making up the lack of the other, a lack which it must necessarily have in order entirely to be what it specifically can be. Then fulfilment is present and the divine is in the midst of the two. Organic, artistic man is the flower of nature, and aorgic nature when it is felt in its purity by the man who is purely organized, purely formed in his fashion, gives him a sense of fulfilment.[17]

Here in substance is the whole of the argument Heidegger deploys on the essence of *technē* defined as a mode – if not the mode – of unconcealing, of *alētheia*, in which one can in fact perceive, especially if one remembers that *technē* is fundamentally language (*Dichtung, Sprache, Sage*: Hölderlin's 'words like flowers') a determination of the apophantic essence of *technē*. This is why it is in fact permissible to think that *mythos* is the most 'archaic' of the *technai* and, secondarily, that the mimetic is always linked to the mythic. But it is, firstly, because *mythos* is 'revealing' in respect of the world and the self, or of peoples, instituting the *as such* of what is (the *self-resembling* of the essent as essent) or uncovering the *that there is* of the essent. In other words, it is initially because *mythos* is naming, in the sense in which Heidegger understands it, and that languages (de)constitute 'subjects', preceding and prescribing them, as the fruits of no 'technical invention' but, like genius (and, moreover, like the genius of peoples, as the expression goes), pure gift of *physis* in infinite excess over its infinite failure to appear or to unconceal itself. (Which clearly establishes that *technē* is (in)human and *unheimlich*.)

Now we may say that Heidegger saw this very clearly from the beginning (I mean from the point of his 'break' with Nazism) and that this is precisely what orientates his thinking right up to the meditation on the essence of technology and language in his last years; and that at the same time something in all this remained hidden from him, as if his brutal exclusion of *mimēsis* had left him an unwitting prisoner of a basically traditonal or, in other words Platonic, mimetology: that mimetology which identifies *technē* with fiction. I can see two indications of this.

On the one hand, it is initially in respect of the work of art that Heidegger seizes upon the word *Gestell* to make it mean the gathering together of all the modes of *stellen* – chief among them, in relation to art, being *Herstellen* (produce), *Darstellen* (present) and *Feststellen* (institute, constitute) – through which he seeks to ground the work in its essence as *truth's being fixed in place in the figure (Festgestelltsein der Wahrheit in die Gestalt).*[18] The semantic chain of *Stellen* does admittedly come into competition, in this passage, which is one of Heidegger's most audacious, with the chain – quite different in scope – of *reissen* (*Riss, Aufriss, Grundriss, Durchriss, Umriss*, etc.), in which one can see the outlines of a thinking of *technē*, and, as a consequence, of difference, on the basis of the incision, the trait or the 'inaugural' tracing, of the breaching/broaching *(entame)* or the inscription – in short, of something not unrelated to the archi-trace or archi-writing in Derrida's sense. The work is, none the less, *Gestalt* or, in other words, *figura*, of the truth and this determination – even if Heidegger certainly does not think in terms of fiction, nor even of imagination – is consistent with the onto-typological theme of the *Rectoral Address* (or of *Vom Wesen des Grundes*) and distributes the roles of 'creators' and 'guardians' of the work, that is to say the division of roles constitutive of the 'mission' of art. That Heidegger

should subsequently have carried over on to modern technology
what, almost twenty years earlier (though in the interim a perhaps
unprecedented 'turnabout' of history had occurred), was seen as
being true of the work of art, and that, parallel with this, he had
taken up again the problematic of the trait (of the *Riss*) in relation
to language, indicates clearly enough what 'political' journey
thought had to make to arrive at the revelation of Nazism in its
'truth'.

Moreover – and this is the second moment when this becomes
clear – it was not until 1955, and the letter to Jünger (*Zur Seinsfrage*
(*The Question of Being*), trans. W. Kluback and J. T. Wilde
(London, Vision Press, 1959)) that Heidegger in fact *denounced*
onto-typology and came to impugn as a mere overturning of
Platonism within the spiritual – historial space of the death of God
and the infinitization of the subject ('rescendence' as against
transcendence) the whole onto-typological thematics of the figure
or build (*Gestalt*), of the stamping and the imprint (*Prägung,
Gepräge*), which had none the less been his since 1933. In other
words, it was not until ten years after the collapse of the Third
Reich that Heidegger had the definitive revelation that National
Socialism (national-Aestheticism) was the truth of the inversion of
Platonism or of the restoration of what Plato had fought against –
though not without yielding to tyranny himself – in other words,
the thinking of the technical or the political as *fiction*: the last
attempt at 'mythizing' the West.[20] Though not, probably, the last
aestheticization of the political.

NOTES

1 'Die Überwindung der Äesthetik in der Frage nach der Kunst' was
   the title of a colloquium co-organized by Heidegger in the Winter
   term of 1935–6, at which he presented the first version of 'The
   Origin of the Work of Art'.
2 This is a subordination that can clearly be seen in the first of
   Heidegger's lectures on Nietzsche, all the more puzzling in that it
   holds Plato responsible for mimetology. As *The Introduction of*

Metaphysics explains, from the moment that it is 'quiddity' and not 'quodditas' – *essentia* and not *existentia* – that determines the essence of Being, 'quiddity' presents itself as 'that which is most beingful in an essent' or 'the actual essent', *ontōs on*. Being understood thus is *idea*, itself interpreted as *paradeigma* in relation to the essent which is now degraded to what Plato calls *mē on*. This is why, as the idea, which 'at the same time . . . necessarily becomes an ideal', 'the copy actually 'is' not; it merely partakes of being, it is a *methexis*'. The *mē on*, the essent, is thought as copy (*Nach-Abbild*) and appearance (*physis, phainomenon*) as 'the emergence of the copy'. I quote, without modification, Ralph Manheim's translation: 'The truth of *physis, alētheia* as the unconcealment that is the essence of the emerging power, now becomes *homoīosis* and *mimēsis*, assimilation and accommodation, orientation by . . . it becomes a correctness of vision, of apprehension as representation' (*An Introduction to Metaphysics* (New Haven/London, Yale University Press, 1964), pp. 184–5).

3 'Being-human defines itself from out of a relation to what is as a whole. The human *essence* shows itself here to be the relation which first opens up Being to man. Being-human as the need [*Not*] of apprehension and collection, is a being-driven [*Nötigung*] into the freedom of undertaking *technē*, the sapient embodiment of being. This is the character of history' (*An Introduction to Metaphysics*, p. 170).

4 See note 18 of the preceding chapter. As ever, Hegel sees all this with perfect clarity. Here for example is the widely celebrated opening passage of his *Lectures on the History of Philosophy*, trans. E. S. Haldane (London, Routledge and Kegan Paul, 1963), vol. 1, pt 1, pp. 149–50:

The name of Greece strikes home to the hearts of men of education in Europe, and more particularly is this so with us Germans. Europeans have taken their religion, the life-to-come, the far-off land, from a point somewhat further off than Greece – they took it from the East, and more especially from Syria. But the here, the present, art and science, that which in giving liberty to our spiritual life gives it dignity as it likewise bestows upon it ornament, we know to have proceeded from Greece either directly or indirectly – through the circuitous road of Rome. The latter of these two ways was the earlier form in which this culture came to us; it also came from the formerly universal church which derived its origin as such from Rome, and has retained its speech even until now. The sources of authority in addition to the Latin Gospels have been the Fathers. Our law, too, boasts of deriving its most perfect forms from Rome. Teutonic strength of mind has required to pass through the hard discipline of the church and law which came to us from Rome, and to be kept in check; it is in this way that the European character first obtained its pliability and capacity for freedom. Thus it was after European manhood came to be at home with itself and to look upon the present, that the historical and that which is of foreign derivation was given. When man began to be at home with himself, he turned to the Greeks to find enjoyment in it. Let us leave the Latin and the Roman to the church and to jurisprudence. Higher, freer, philosophic science, as also the beauty of our untrammelled art, the taste for, the love of the same we know to have taken their root in Greek life and to have created therefrom their spirit. If we were to have an aspiration, it would be for such a land and such conditions.

Moreover, Hegel – I here point out in anticipation – associates precisely this theme of Greece as 'native land' with *autochthony*. Evoking the birth of the Greek spirit, Hegel (like the Nietzsche of the *Untimely Meditations* on history, as Sarah Kofman rightly points out to me) concedes that the Greeks 'have certainly more or less received the rudiments of their religion, culture and their social consensus from Asia, Syria and Egypt; but they have effaced, transformed, elaborated, overturned what of this origin was foreign to them, they have metamorphosed the latter, so that what they, like us, have appreciated, recognized and loved, is essentially theirs'. And he adds, a few lines later: 'They have thus not only themselves created the substantial in their culture (the foreign origin they have so to speak thanklessly forgotten, putting it in the background – perhaps burying it in the darkness of the mysteries which they have kept secret from themselves), they have not only made their existence their own, but they have also held in reverence this their spiritual rebirth, which is their real birth' (ibid., pp. 150–1). This is of course something of an exhortation and goes some way to explaining the profound relatedness of the Greeks and the Germans. The tropism of the 'at home' is the sign of such a relatedness and it finds its natural resting place in philosophy:

But what makes us specially at home with the Greeks is that they made their world their home; the common spirit of homeliness unities us both. In ordinary life, we like best the men and families that are homely and contented in themselves, not desiring what is outside and above them . . . (ibid., p. 150).

It is in this veritable homeliness, or, more accurately, in the spirit of homeliness, in this spirit of ideally being-at-home-with-themselves in their physical, corporate, legal, moral and political existence; it is in the beauty and the freedom of their character in history, making what they are to be also a sort of Mnemosyne with them, that the kernel of thinking liberty rests; and hence it was requisite that Philosophy should arise amongst them. Philosophy is being at home with self, just like the homeliness of the Greek; it is man's being at home in his mind, at home with himself. (Ibid, pp. 151–2)

Just as Hegel re-works the theme of autochthony speculatively, so he also resolves the final oxymoron in favour of the universal (of spirit), of the 'free of all particularity' (the 'at-home' has no other site than the spirit) – which is something the 'thinking of finitude' obviously will not do. The recognition of such a 'at home' is none the less, something specifically Graeco-German: Fichte had already proclaimed it and Heidegger will do more than merely remember it (Hegel, *Lectures on the History of Philosophy*, pt 1, 'Greek Philosophy', pp. 149ff).

   One must also note that, out of all the slogans of the 'Conservative Revolution' of the 1930s, the rejection of 'Romanness' is the one which characterizes Niekisch's 'National Bolshevism' (towards which, for example, Jünger was by no means hostile), in its very opposition to the 'fascisms' of the Latin Catholic countries (a hostility, moreover, that Heidegger very clearly shares).

5 This tradition is coherently expressed in the 1930s in the work of Walter F. Otto. See, in particular, his *The Homeric Gods*, trans. Moses Hadas (New York, Pantheon, 1954). We may note, in passing, that Otto was an 'opponent' of the regime – or at least of its official ideology – as were all the founders of, and contributors to, *die Geistige Überlieferung* (Reinhardt, Grassi, Heidegger, Furtwängler, etc.).

6 This model is explicitly Heidegger's in the *Rectoral Address*.

7 Otto, *The Homeric Gods*, p. 10.

8 I am not, by speaking of schizophrenia, endorsing the 'pathological' version of Nazism here. If Nazism is a spiritual–historical 'illness', then at the very least we must say that the illness was already in existence before and only reached its moment of crisis in Nazism. As for the essential thrust of my remarks here, I am following the insights offered in Thomas Mann's *Doktor Faustus* and the work of Uwe Johnson.

9 *Group Psychology and the Analysis of the Ego*, Standard Edition (London, Hogarth, 1959), vol. 18.

10 Philippe Lacoue-Labarthe and Jean-Luc Nancy, 'La panique politique', *Confrontations* 2, (1979); and 'Le peuple juif ne rêve pas', in *La psychanalyse est-elle une histoire juive?* (Paris, Le Seuil, 1981).

11 In which case Marx, who was merciless towards imitative historical repetitions (cf. *The eighteenth Brumaire of Louis Bonaparte*), and scarcely showed any affection for those 'children' of humanity, the Greeks (cf. *Contribution to the Critique of Political Economy*) is the proof of the very profound 'health' of Hegel.

12 *The Question of Being*, trans. William Kluback and Jean T. Wilde (London, Vision Press, 1959).

13 'Désistance', preface to the American edition of *Typography* (Boston, Mass., Harvard University Press, 1988.

14 'Le mythe individuel du névrosé ou "poésie et vérité dans la névrose"', *Ornicar?* (May, 1979).

15 Quoted in Adolphe Reinach, *La Peinture ancienne (Recueil Milliet)*, ed. Agnès Rouveret (Paris, Macula, 1985), pp. 54–7. As Suzanne Saïd points out, 'as old as' is not perhaps the best translation. But neither is it the most erroneous. However we see this, this proposition is seeking to stress the co-originarity of *physis* and *technē*. This is, I remain convinced, the basis of Greek thought. And it is precisely this that Hölderlin and Hegel recovered from oblivion, that they *discovered*.

16 'You see, dear Brother, that I have presented you with a paradox: the urge to create art and culture . . . is a true service which men render to nature' (Hölderlin, letter to his brother, 4 June 1799, in *Sämtliche Werke*, (Stuttgart, Kohlhammer, 1964), vol. 6, pp. 328–9.

17 'Grund des Empedokles', *Sämtliche Werke* vol. 4, p. 152. [My translation, C.T.]

18 'The Origin of the Work of Art', p. 64.

19 Philippe Lacoue-Labarthe and Jean-Luc Nancy, 'Le mythe nazi', in *Les mécanismes du fascisme* (Colloque de Schiltigheim, Strasbourg, 1980).

20 I borrow the term – perhaps bending it somewhat to my own ends –
    from Jean-Luc Nancy (*la Communauté désoeuvrée*), if only to mark
    my total solidarity with the theme of the 'interruption of myth'
    which is also for me, via Celan, that of the interruption of art (*La
    Poésie comme expérience* (Paris, Christian Bourgois Editeur, 1986)).

9

The Fiction of the Political

The political transformation which occurred in Heidegger's 'late work' could be analysed on its own account, and I think we would find that the dialogue Heidegger struck up again with Hannah Arendt would certainly have some part to play in this. I cannot, however, go into this matter here. On the other hand, I believe it is absolutely essential that I indicate – in order to clarify matters – what it was that Heidegger was breaking with when he broke with Jünger. My hypothesis is that it was with nothing less than the political fiction of the German myth, i.e. with something which in spite of everything (in spite of the huge gulf regarding the thinking of Being which separated the two) was very close to what might be defined as the Nazi myth.

By 'Nazi myth', I do not mean the reactivation of any particular myth (whether Germanic, Indo-European or other) which Nazism might be seen as having incorporated into the programme of its ideology or its propaganda, nor even the elevation of *mythos* (as against *logos* or *ratio*) which formed the basic essentials of the 'thinking' of Krieck or Baümler. This reassertion of the value of myth is not foreign to the construction of the Nazi myth (nor is it absent from Heidegger's thinking); it is, however, only a consequence of it. That is to say that it is only an effect of Nazism's desire to mythify, or, in other words, of the desire, for Nazism (the movement and later the State), to present itself as myth or as realization of a myth (setting myth to work and breathing life into it). In this sense, as is perfectly clear from a reading of Rosenberg,[1] myth is in no way 'mythological'. It is a 'power' (*puissance*), the power that is in the gathering together of the fundamental forces and orientations of an individual or a people, that is to say the power of a deep, concrete, embodied identity. Rosenberg interprets this power as that of the dream, as the projection of an image with which one identifies through a total and immediate commitment. Such an image is in no way a product of 'fabulation', to which myth is ordinarily reduced; it is the figuration of a *type* conceived both as a model of identity and as that identity formed and realized. And this type in its turn provides the myth with its truth in that it allows the dream to lay hold of 'the whole man'. When Rosenberg writes that today (in 1930) 'we (Germans) are beginning to dream again our original dreams', he is thinking neither of Wotan nor Odin (Odin is dead, he says), but of the essence of the Germanic soul (which is the resurrection of Odin) in so far as it, like the Greek soul which was itself also Aryan, dreams the political (honour and the State) as *Formwillen*, the desire to form and the desire for form or *Gestaltung*: as *work*.

Naturally, this onto-typological interpretation of myth fits in with a racism: the Germanic soul is here that of a race which is only as it is by virtue of its belonging to blood and soil, and nothing of the frenzied (and 'scientific') incorporation of the echo of Greek autochthony is left out, not even the dream of being begotten by the father alone. But racism is a consequence of the onto-typology, not its cause: 'The freedom of the soul', explains Rosenberg, 'is *Gestalt*. The *Gestalt* is always limited in its form. This limitation (which outlines the figure, traces the contours of the type) is conditioned by race. But this race is the external figure of a determinate soul.' In other words, race (and such is the content of the myth: myth is the myth of the race) is the identity of a formative power, of a type, or, in other words, of a bearer of myth. This perfect circularity, in which we can recognize that *tautegory* Schelling borrowed from Coleridge, means nothing less than this: the myth (of the race) is the myth of myth, or the myth of the formative power of myths. It is the myth of 'mythopoiesis' itself, of which the type, by the very logic of aesthetico-political immanentism, is both productive of and produced by fiction. Moreover, this is why myth, signifying nothing other than itself, is a product of pure self-formation and finds its truth or its verification as the self-foundation of the people (or the race: the

translation of the word *völkisch* is, in fact, undecidable) in confor-
mity with its type. Equally, in the onto-typology thus arrived at,
it is the ontology of subjectivity (of the will to will) that finds its
fulfilment. Nazism is the Nazi myth, i.e. the Aryan type, as
absolute subject, pure will (of the self) willing itself.

Several consequences follow from this:

(1)   Ideology can no more be seen as a means to an end – for
example as a 'propaganda technique' – than can the various forms
of performance that generate an experience of fusion. The self-
production of the Aryan myth is an end in itself, the end as
immanent, embodied and immediate (Rosenberg, who constantly
uses the term *Erlebnis* calls it a 'lived') realization of the self-
identity of the people or the race. The end here is pure commitment to and participation in the myth and the type: 'The life of a
race', writes Rosenberg, . . . is the formation of a mystic synth-
esis'. It is wrong to reduce fascism, as is often done, to a mass
manipulation technique. Fascism is, rather, the mobilization of the
identificatory emotions of the masses.

(2)   The awakening of the power of myth – the auto-poietic act –
becomes a necessity once the inconsistency of the abstract univer-
sals of reason has been revealed and the beliefs of modern
humanity (Christianity and belief in humanity itself), which were
at bottom only bloodless myths, have collapsed. But here again
we should be careful: Nazism is a humanism in so far as it rests
upon a determination of *humanitas* which is, in its view, more
powerful – i.e. more effective – than any other. The subject of
absolute self-creation, even if, occupying an immediately natural
position (the particularity of the race), it transcends all the
determinations of the modern subject, brings together and con-
cretizes these same determinations (as also does Stalinism with the
subject of absolute self-production) and constitutes itself as *the*
subject, in absolute terms. The fact that this subject lacks the
universality which apparently defines the *humanitas* of humanism
in the received sense, still does not make Nazism an anti-
humanism. It simply situates it within the logic, of which there are

many other examples, of the realization and the becoming-concrete of 'abstractions'.

(3)   The Jews do not belong to *humanitas* thus defined because they have neither dreams nor myths. Maurice Blanchot is right when he says 'the Jews embody . . . the rejection of myths, the eschewing of idols, the recognition of an ethical order which manifests itself in respect for the law. What Hitler is attempting to annihilate in annihilating the Jew, and the "myth of the Jew", is precisely man liberated from myths.'[2] This 'rejection of myths' is precisely what explains why the Jews do not constitute a type: they have, says Rosenberg, no *Seelengestalt* – and therefore no *Rassengestalt*. They are a formless, unaesthetic 'people', which by definition cannot enter into the process of self-fictioning and cannot constitute a subject, or, in other words, a being-proper (*être-propre*). It is this unassignable (and formidable) im-properness of the Jews which makes them, says Rosenberg once again, not the direct opposite (a counter-type) of the Teuton, but his contradiction – the very absence of type. Hence their power – they who are neither *Kulturbegründer* nor *Kulturschöpfer*, but mere *Kulturträger*, bearers of civilization – to insert themselves into every culture and State and then to live a life that is parasitic upon these, constantly threatening them with bastardization. All in all, the Jews are infinitely mimetic beings, or, in other words, the site of an *endless mimesis*, which is both interminable and inorganic, producing no art and achieving no appropriation. They are destabilization itself.

This is just one example, summarized here rather cursorily, of Nazi onto-typology.

It is immediately easy to see the features which make it *absolutely* impossible to confuse this schema with Jünger's argument on the *Gestalt* of the Worker, and, *a fortiori*, with the arguments of Heidegger – who moreover never troubled to conceal his contempt for Rosenberg – concerning the work of art, *Dichtung*, the people and history. It becomes all the more impossible to do so when one takes into account that this presentation credits Rosenberg with a coherence and a philosophical logic which are, in fact, totally absent from his work. *The Myth of the Twentieth Century* is a repetitive, jargon-ridden, barely readable hotch-potch of a book which belongs to that vein of authoritarian, voluntaristic logor-rhea that formed the 'style' of the period and consists merely in noisy, stereotyped assertions. By no stretch of the imagination could it be confused with the work of Jünger or Heidegger, and, in any case, its anti-semitism renders it absolutely incompatible with their writings.

It is none the less the case that from a certain elevated vantage point, the one which our positionless position in history today gives us and the fact that in May 1968 (which was a political experience of which we have yet to feel all the – more than merely political-consequences) there was a clear-sighted renunciation of the archaeo-politics which would inevitably reconstitute itself sooner or later (in its hard revolutionary form; and it seemed better in the end to allow the restoration of the only more or less liveable political reality – with all its banal and, no less inevitable, burden of compromise – that had stubbornly survived through the catastrophic fulfilments of the Western political project)[3], from this lofty vantage point, then, it is nonetheless the same thing that is basically seeking expression in various quarters. From an even loftier height, that 'same thing' is perhaps contained in the oft-cited and indeed memorable sentence Thucydides attributes to Pericles in his *Funeral Oration*:

φιλοχαλοῦμεν τε γὰρ μετ' ευτελδιαζ χαὶ φιλοσουμεν ανευ μαλαχίας

This sentence is generally considered untranslatable. Jacqueline de Romilly suggests: 'We cultivate the beautiful in its simplicity, and the things of the mind, without losing our firmness.'[4] This is playing safe, but the term 'cultivate' has a Latin ring to it that is quite foreign to the text. Hannah Arendt, by contrast, takes a very great risk: 'We are lovers of beauty within the limits of political judgement [*euteleia,* understood as precision of intention would here be understood as the very essence of political 'virtue'], and we philosophize without the Barbarian vice of softness'.[5] For his part, Cornelius Castoriadis, who considers this reference to political judgement improbable, paraphrases as follows: 'We have our being in and through the love of beauty and wisdom and the activity to which this love gives rise. We live by, with and through these things, but fleeing extravagance and softness'.[6]

I shall opt for a literal translation. 'We love the beautiful with frugality and knowledge without softness.' 'Frugality' here is an economic category:[7] *euteleia* has never signified rightness of judgement, political or otherwise, but simplicity of means deployed. It is the absence of luxury, of pomp – and, first and foremost, of expenditure. In other words, it is rigour, if not indeed austerity. On the other hand, *malakia* certainly does mean 'softness', which is in fact the supreme Barbarian vice, i.e. the Oriental vice. Pericles' (and Thucydides') utterance celebrates the heroism – the *bearing* – in the combined practice of art and thought, which he knew he had raised to unsurpassed heights, of that 'haughty little people' as Nietzsche would call them, in the face of an adversity they had to confront without resources. Exposed to distress (*Not*), as Heidegger would say in the 1930s, identifying Germany with Greece and calling upon it, with all the force of *technē* (art and knowledge) to rise up against the overpowering force of the concealment of the essent.

How then could we not see that in this utterance, which brings together art and philosophy to say what constitutes the specific quality and the heroic singularity of the Athenian *polis*, there is, not the founding charter of our 'democracies', but the programme of something which had an horrific fulfilment of which we are, so to speak, the definitively caesura-ed heirs?

NOTES

1   Philippe Lacoue-Labarthe and Jean-Luc Nancy, 'Le mythe nazi' in *Les mecanismes du fascisme* (Colloque de Schiltigheim, Strasbourg, 1980). What follows is based upon the analyses that appear there. The reading of Rosenberg's *Myth of the Twentieth Century* and Hitler's *Mein Kampf* is the work of Jean-Luc Nancy, whose analysis I follow here.

2 'Les intellectuels en question', *Le Débat* (33, May 1984).

3 I also wish to express here my profound agreement with the pages Maurice Blanchot devoted to May 1968 in *La Communauté inavouable* (Paris, Minuit, 1983) and *Michel Foucault tel que je l'imagine* (Paris, Fata Morgana, 1986).

4 Thucydides, *La Guerre du Péloponnèse, Bk II, XL* (Paris, les Belles Lettres, 1967), p. 29.

5 Patrick Lévy (ed.), *La Crise de la culture* (Paris Gallimard, 1972), pp. 273–4.

6 'La Polis grecque et la création de la démocratie', in *Domaines de l'homme [Les Carrefours du Labyrinthe II]* (Paris, Seuil, 1986), p. 305.

7 I am indebted to Suzanne Saïd for this piece of information.

Postscript

For a third and last time, I take the liberty of responding to a number of objections that have been levelled against me.

One of these, to begin with the simplest, is the product of a misreading. How can anyone possibly conclude from my rehearsal of Rosenberg's theses on myth in the immediately foregoing pages, or even from the fact that, after quoting Blanchot, I translate Rosenberg into my own terms, that I am making Rosenberg's arguments about the Jews my own? My translation ('All in all, the Jews are infinitely mimetic beings . . .' has no other purpose than to emphasize the presence of the philosophical cultural *stereotype* which one finds, for example, in Nietzsche, in the celebrated aphorism known as 'The Problem of the Actor'. As for the Blanchot phrase, it so happens that it expresses a precise understanding of the reason why the Nazis – and Rosenberg foremost among them – called for the persecution and elimination of the Jews. It seemed to me this was obvious.

This misunderstanding connects with another, which is similar in nature. On several occasions, I stress the fact, which is indeed well-known, that in National Socialist ideology or even, more broadly, in what might still in many respects be termed German ideology*, Judaism (which is sometimes even associated with Christianity) is a 'foreign body' for European culture, i.e. for originally Greek or Graeco-Latin culture. This again is a stereotype and, moreover, connects with the other mentioned above. But, here again, why should anyone think I am making it mine? Certainly I may suspect, against certain crudely reductionist arguments, that the God who is being addressed in certain Judaic traditions and on whom the believers meditate, has 'evaded capture by the Hellenistic and Roman traditions', as I say in chapter 4. Then again, it is perfectly obvious that, massively (that is to say, as a mass phenomenon), anti-semitism is a consequence of the Christian culture which dominated Europe for centuries (I shall return to this point). Yet, for all this, I do not in any sense

*A reference to Marx's work *Die deutsche Ideologie*, idiosyncratically translated into English as *The* German Ideology [translator's note].

subscribe to the 'proper/own body' ('corps propre') thesis because, for one thing, (and it is not the only one) I do not subscribe to the thesis of European identity nor to that of the homogeneity of the West, nor indeed to that of the unicity–singularity of the History of Being. One should not attribute to me the positions I am analysing. My 'Heideggerianism' in no way prevents me from thinking, amongst other things, that there are at least other scansions in the History of Being than those indicated by Heidegger and other trajectories in the constitution of the philosophical than those which Heidegger re-marks after Hegel. In fact – and here again I thought this was clearly visible – it is the idea of *organicity* that I am problematizing and, behind it, that of properness (*propriété*): I no more believe in the phantasy of a 'proper/own body' of Europe, than I do in the fiction of the people as work of art.

However, just as things that I reject are imputed to me, intentions are ascribed to me which I do not have. For example (but it is more than an example), though it is not suggested that I am re-tracing the genesis of Nazism (it is clear that my approach is not that of the historian), I am none the less assumed to be researching into its origins or offering an explanatory schema. And it is then objected that the technical transformation of work and social control is a more important factor than anti-semitism; or that the phenomenon of anti-semitism in its turn remains inexplicable if it is taken in isolation from the religious history of Europe, from several centuries of Lutheran teaching and Jesuit influence (which can even be found in the backgrounds of the Nazi leaders), in which case, here again, the sacrificial logic of the Extermination is said to have escaped me. In this way, I am credited with wishing, though my 'Greek model' (which smacks rather of academicism) and my question of art (is this not aestheticism?), to provide a purely philosophical explanation of Nazism, which is, naturally, extremely fragile and tendentious, if not indeed thoroughly scandalous (I am said to have traced a direct line from Pericles to Hitler and to have laid all the blame upon Athens, which was in fact the home of democracy, as if my ultimate intention were to exculpate Christianity).

I should like to reply briefly to all these points.

Even if I remain convinced that there is much to be said about
Pericles' Funeral Oration (on this subject, see Nichole Loraux's
work) and thus on Athenian democracy, I do not for a moment
consider this document a programme for Nazism (nor do I see
Pericles as prefiguring Hitler, though surely this hardly needs
saying). I simply take from it one single sentence, the echo of
which, as it seems to me, was to resonate after more than two
thousand years in a certain German thinking which was inhabited
to the point of obsession by the 'Greek model' and was not far
removed from what unfolded – or rather from what, to a great
extent, failed to unfold itself – in National Socialism. I use the
term 'programme' here with some confidence and I am thinking
in fact of a sort of 'ideological programme'. Not that Nazi
ideology is attributable to some 'master thinker' or other. But
Nazism was heir to a 'philosophical' legacy, deformed and degraded as it may have been, the importance and dimensions of
which have, I believe, been underestimated. Hitler might have
called Himmler 'our Ignatius Loyola', but this did not mean that
he had not also read Nietzsche, after his own fashion; and if he had
feasted on Karl May (another 'source'?), he had also been intoxi-
cated with Wagner. As is attested by the art, architecture, cere-
monial and town planning of the Third Reich – or *a contrario* by a
solid hostility to the Church – the 'Greek reverie' which for more
than a hundred years had had its place in that country's school and
university curricula was extremely powerful in 1930's Germany.

Having said this, my 'Greek model' (which is, by the way,
more the model of Greece before Pericles and the appearance of
democracy) is not an 'explanation' of Nazism and anti-semitism.
It is, as Heidegger's *critical* discourse towards Nazism reveals, a
truth of Nazism that was buried and that did not reveal itself (or
did so only partially) but which was none the less active *as such*.
This is why I believe it is possible to discern a national-
aestheticism beneath National Socialism (a national-aestheticism
which, moreover, I at no point attribute to Heidegger, as critics
have tried to make out: Heidegger was precisely the first, just after
the 'break', to attack aesthetics, that is to say, the whole of the
Western philosophy of art, and to attempt to re-pose the question of
art on quite other bases). The fact that this national-aestheticism,

imperfectly detached as it was from the 'scientific' farrago weighing it down (but, ultimately, Heidegger also showed that in Nietzsche aestheticism and biologism are inextricably mingled), entered in a decisive way into the Hitlerian variant of anti-semitism is something I continue to believe, without for all that believing that this 'explains' the mass phenomenon of anti-semitism.[1] If one prefers, there is no question here of a *cause*. This is why I speak, for want of a better term, in terms of *essences*.

As for the essence, then, my intuition is that *imitation* (that is to say what metaphysics understands by this term) is decisive in the formation of the modern political sphere. And that, moreover, this too is perhaps an archaism, a leftover from Plutarch, which means perhaps that there is no truly modern politics.[2] This is a difficulty, it seems to me, which Heidegger recognized. Hence his complex strategy towards the 'Greek beginning' (though I do not believe that this succeeds in extricating itself from mimetic logic); hence also his disillusioned remark in the *Spiegel* interview, when he says that he is not convinced that democracy is the political form that best corresponds to the Age of Technology. Unlike a good number of my contemporaries for whom democracy is sacred, I believe the difficulty remains and that it still faces us today. And if I think that, in the absence of any other 'model' which does not imply instituting some form of terror or enslave-ment, democracy is today 'the only more or less liveable political reality', this does not prevent me from remaining convinced that we should not at any point cease to question democracy merely on the pretext that we do not have (too many) police breathing down our necks or that our labour is not (too) exploited.

1   Or, for all that, seeking to absolve Christianity of blame. Since it is in part to him that these remarks are addressed, I refer the reader to Jean-Joseph Goux, 'Freud et la structure religieuse du nazisme', *Les Iconoclastes* (Paris, Le Seuil, 1978), with whose arguments I am broadly in agreement.

2   Though I do not share the epistemological assumptions of his work nor, doubtless, all his conclusions, I am in agreement on this point with the analysis proposed by Jean-Claude Milner in 'Science, politique, savoirs' (*Bulletin de la Société francaise de philosophie* 80 (4) (October – December 1986).

10

The Task of Thinking

In what were certainly rather dubious, if not indeed thoroughly painful circumstances, Adorno wrote one day that Heidegger's 'philosophy is fascist right down to its most intimate components'.[1] Adorno, who was on the defensive, was perhaps forced into exaggeration here. But it is well known that even in his more intemperate moments, his remarks often struck the target. Let us convert this dogmatic (and peremptory) affirmation into a question. For a real question does arise here. It might be formulated as follows: What do the commitment of 1933, the paucity of his explanations, the absence of any disavowal, and his silence on the Extermination (and the responsibility of Germany or Europe) do to the philosophy or the thought of Heidegger? Do they merely cast a local, passing shadow upon a body of thought that is otherwise intact and basically uncompromised? Or do they tarnish that thought irremediably to the point that it might be termed, in all essentials, 'fascist'? By not speaking out – or at least saying very little – by refusing to become involved in polemics that were (or would have been) necessarily undignified and violent, by cloaking himself on each occasion in a sort of outraged dignity or by pleading the immeasurable elevation of thought, Heidegger in fact took on a terrible responsibility in respect of his own thinking, which is to say in respect of what he himself called *thought*. He quite simply made an accusation like Adorno's possible. And he also made possible the remark (whether delivered sneeringly or indignantly) that the appeal to the 'task (*tâche*) of thought' was not able – or only barely able – to hide the stain (*tache*) upon thought. And yet he was the first to claim for thought an immense 'historial' responsibility, a responsibility co-extensive with its impotence in the field of immediate action. Was it not Heidegger, replying to Wisser in a televised interview which he had agreed to give on the occasion of his eightieth birthday, who laid emphasis, in his closing remarks, upon the 'task of thinking'[2] (he was referring to the lecture which is precisely entitled 'The End of Philosophy and the Task of Thinkinng' (1964). He concluded, not without emphasis, 'A thinker yet to come who will perhaps one day approach the task of effectively assuming that thinking for which I am attempting to lay the ground, will have to come to terms with something Heinrich von Kleist once wrote: "I stand aside for one who is not yet here and I bow, over a distance of a thousand years, before his mind." ' When you measure things on such a scale, you know what it means to speak of a legacy or heritage in thought. At least you should know that it is rather scabrous to hope to be able to get away with mere silence or a few vague allusions on the lines of 'He who thinks greatly must err greatly'. That being said, for Adorno's accusation to hit its mark, or even for there to be a suspicion that it might, at least two conditions have to be fulfilled:

1   we must know what fascism is in its essence;
2   we must show what *effective* relation there is between the accused (or suspect) 'philosophy' – also in its essence – and a fascism rigorously delimited in this way.

As for the first of these conditions, it is not certain that Adorno was the best placed to satisfy it: beyond merely wielding the word as an insult, what did he mean exactly by 'fascism'? If he simply meant the empirical–historical reality of Nazism, then the accusation would not hold for a moment, unless one were quite dishonestly to conflate Heidegger's writings with those of Rosenberg (or Krieck or Bäumler or so many others of even lesser stature). And unless one were – equally dishonestly – to ignore the accepted evidence of the extent to which Heidegger distanced himself after 1933 – 4 from the regime and its ideology, even if one were only to judge by the first published editions of his lectures from the 1930s (*Introduction to Metaphysics*; *Nietzsche*). Or did

Adorno possess a concept of fascism which was fascism's truth and which, in particular, made it possible to detect it in places where it was not self-evidently present: in the thinking of Being, for example? This is precisely what is in doubt, in so far as Adorno's 'critique' of fascism never freed itself from its Marxist or para-Marxist presuppositions and therefore revealed itself incapable of reaching the place where, a long way this side of their reciprocal hostility (which was in fact irreducible), and therefore a long way this side of 'ideological' or 'political' divergences or oppositions, the ontological – historial co-belonging of Marxism and fascism – or if one prefers, at another ('methodological') level of sociologism and biologism – can be established. Perhaps Adorno, who was eager as could be to speak about it, said less about fascism than did Heidegger in the very parsimony of his declarations (or in the stubborn determination with which, during the fascist years, he attempted to indicate where the truth and the lost or ruined 'inner greatness' of the National Socialist revolution lay). However necessary the political struggle may be, as has frequently been proved, it can obscure the analysis. This in no way means that one should become involved in any 'rehabilitation' or 're-evaluation' of fascism. It simply means that it would be better to learn to stop considering fascism a 'pathological' phenomenon (from what extra-social position, asked Freud, might one make such a diagnosis?) and recognize in it not only (at least) one of the age's possible political forms – and one no more aberrant or inadequate than any other – but the political form that is perhaps best able to bring us enlightenment regarding the essence of modern politics. But quite naturally Adorno wanted to have nothing of that. And, after all, that is something one can *also* understand.

The second condition is even more difficult to satisfy, if only because it depends on the first being satisfied. To sustain the accusation against Heidegger to the end, Adorno would at least have had to mobilize, as Breton did in relation to Bataille, a hyperbolic concept comparable with that of 'superfascism' (*surfascisme*). Now, to my knowledge, he never produced anything of the kind, and he generally contented himself with a denunciation of Heidegger's reactionary 'phraseology' (as others busied themselves with

finding the traces of a set of conservative-revolutionary or agra-
rian themes, etc.). And, having regard to philosophical *and*
political analysis, this is manifestly insufficient. Not that the concept of 'superfascism' (if it is a concept) is not itself problematical.
But it at least had the merit, at the time when it was applied, of
implicitly acknowledging a difference between thought (in this
case Bataille's) and real fascism.

Beneath Adorno's insult, the real question still remains, then,
the following: did fundamental ontology and the analytics of
Dasein harbour within them the possibility of a commitment to
fascism? And if so, to what sort of fascism?

It will always be possible to demonstrate from this perspective
that in effect, not for reasons of some kind of existential–heroic
pathos, but on purely philosophical grounds, it was possible for
him to commit himself to a movement that was national and
popular (I would happily say a national-populism, but the connotations of the term might be misleading).

These philosophical reasons are essentially twofold: firstly, the
relatively secondary and rather cursory treatment of the analytics
of *Mitsein (Being and Time*, paras 25–7), even if Being-with and
Dasein-with are defined as structures of *Dasein* that are 'existentially
constitutive for Being-in-the-world' ('Being-with-one-another', as
the very index of finitude, ultimately remains univestigated except
in partial relations which do not include the great and indeed
overarching division of love and hatred); and, secondly, a certain
overdetermination of historial *Dasein*, co-extensive with its re-
legation to a secondary place, by the concept (itself also unques-
tioned) of 'people' (*Volk*), as can be clearly seen in the paragraphs
relating to history (72–7).[4] It is not even necessary to say, as
Löwith does, that between 1927 and 1933 Heidegger inflected the
ontology of *Jemeinigkeit* or that he 'translated' the *je eigenes Dasein*
as *deutsches Dasein*.[5] At best, he made that translation explicit:
Gemeinwesen was always for Heidegger that of a people, and his
analysis of historiality has no meaning if it is not seen against this
horizon.[6]

It would be much more ambitious, on the other hand, to try
to show that the same fundamental ontology or the same
analytic of *Dasein* could lead to a commitment of a 'socialist' type.

Preoccupations that might properly be termed 'social' are not absent from *Sein und Zeit* (Bourdieu felt inspired to translate these 'into ordinary language', which is to say that he quite simply wrested them away from fundamental ontology, which for the purpose, he had reduced to an overblown, authoritarian and self-sacralizing phraseology).[7] Nothing, however, prefigures the type of ontology of labour which is developed in certain of the procla-mations of 1933–4 (though, as I have indicated, this lasts only for the period of his commitment *stricto sensu* to Nazism). And the theme of technology, as we know, only appears after the 'turn' (*Kehre*), in a context in which hostility to National Socialism is explicit and declared (the last pages of the *Introduction to Metaphysics*).

To accuse Heidegger's philosophy, before his political commit-ment of 1933, of being 'fascist right down to its most intimate components' can only be a charge produced by superficiality or ill-will, if fascism is defined, in its German form, as National Socialism. That philosophy is, admittedly, opposed to any idea of internationalism, rationalism (but *also* irrationalism), humanism, progressism, etc.; it rails against the *Aufklärung* (though it does so in terms of the Kantian theme of finitude); but it also manages to wrest itself free, though with some difficulty, from the subjectivistic–voluntaristic ontology of the latest metaphysics (which happens to be Nietzsche's). If one has to provide a political definition, it can be said to be a heroico-tragic *and* revolutionary philosophy 'of the Right'. It could there-fore, in the effectively revolutionary circumstances of 1933, allow scope, *volens nolens* (or rather at the cost of a certain number of serious – philosophically serious – compromises) for a political commitment, by which I mean something more than mere support. But everything about it – or almost everything – ran counter to that commitment being a lasting one (I would not say quite so much for the support), once the (immodest and naive) illusion had passed that the movement might be open in some way to possible 'entryism'.[8] And in fact, so far as the essentials of Nazism's *metaphysical* positions were concerned, the break was inevitable.

Could one therefore speak of a sort of 'archi-fascism'? Perhaps so, but here again two conditions would have to be fulfilled: (1) that biologism and racism be eliminated from fascism in its Hitlerian version (which seems relatively difficult to say the least); (2) that the *archi* in archi-fascism be understood not in its metaphysical sense (priority, principle, overarching instance etc.). Which may be appropriate, as I have tried to show elsewhere, if we restrict ourselves to Heidegger's ten months as Rector, but is not at all appropriate afterwards, i.e. after the 'break', for the very simple reason that the 'break' and the determination of Nazism's truth (or of the truth to which it could not accede) is exactly contemporaneous with the abandonment of *fundamental* ontology. And therefore contemporaneous, as is still generally forgotten, with the *Kehre* itself (whether one likes it or not, Heidegger's sudden lurch into politics threw his own thinking into a very severe crisis). To argue, as I believe one can, that Heidegger's discourse on art contains the truth of what I call national-aestheticism, does not mean for a moment that Nazism could have recognized itself in that discourse or risen to its heights: in its very principle – for reasons, that is, which relate to its very definition (its all-out technicism, for example) – it precisely could not (it is just this failure which Heidegger pointed out to it). But this also does not mean that Heidegger was hoping, by that discourse, to give fascism a 'good image', nor, even less, to 'correct distortions of it', since he knew, as early as the 'break' (and doubtless also before, which is where he committed a wrong) that fascism – like Marxism and 'Americanism' – resulted from a misapprehension, which in this case was fundamental, regarding the essence of *technē*. In short, we could not speak of 'archi-fascism' if Heidegger himself had not taught us to think philosophically, what fascism, plain and simple, is about. One should re-read here the notes extracted from Heidegger's *Beiträge* and published in *The End of Philosophy* as 'Overcoming Metaphysics'. Who in our age has said so much and so much of such 'profundity' on fascism – and, consequently on our 'world'?[9]

Of all the political themes that make up the politically committed discourse of 1933–4, only one, as we know, was not subsequently disowned (but this was in actual fact a theme that pre-dated the commitment to Nazism since it underlay his *Inaugural*

Address of 1929 at Freiburg), the theme of the University. Right up
to his final years (in the interview he granted to *Der Spiegel* in 1966
and his television appearance with Wisser in 1969), Heidegger was
eager to remind his listeners that his 'programme' was contained –
negatively – in this single proposition (from 'What is Metaphysics'
(1929)):

> The fields of the sciences are very far removed from one another.
> Their manner of treating their objects is radically different. These
> multiple, disparate disciplines owe their cohesion today solely to the
> technical organization of the universities and the faculties and only
> retain their meaning by virtue of the practical goals of the disciplines
> themselves. By contrast, the rooting of the sciences in their essential
> ground is long dead.[10]

Transcribed, retrospectively, into the register of 'entryism', this
same argument becomes:

> It runs counter to the facts to argue that National Socialism and the
> Party had assigned no spiritual goal to the University and the
> concept of science. They had decided that goal only too *categorically*,
> drawing on Nietzsche, in whose doctrine truth does not have its
> own ground and content, but is merely a means employed by will to
> power, i.e. a mere idea, a subjective representation. What was
> grotesque in this, and remains so, was that this concept of a 'political
> science' is in principle consonant with the conception of ideas and
> ideology in Marxism and Communism.
>
> My *Rectoral Address* ... is quite clearly and explicitly directed
> *against this*. And I formulated these positions openly *for the University
> and against the vocational college [Fachschule]* shortly afterwards at the
> Erfurt Congress. I spoke then spontaneously and passionately
> *against* the vocational college and *for* the University which must have
> the Faculty of Philosophy and the Sciences as its support (*tragende
> Mitte*). The division at the time was not between:
> the old university Association on the one hand and the Nazi party on
> the other;
> Reaction on one side and the Revolution on the other, but between
> (conceived in terms of their basic principles):
> the vocational college on the one hand and the University on the
> other.[11]

Mutatis mutandis, it has to be said that this is still the situation now. As had been known in Germany since Kant and Humboldt – and as, of course, is no longer known there (though it is the same everywhere) – the problem of the University is not an incidental or peripheral problem of Western societies, but their central, prime problem, at least if one grants that the West defines itself on the basis of knowledge and *technē*, or, more exactly, of knowledge as *technē*. (Something of this was touched upon in May 1968, in spite of the Marxizing or Freudo-Marxizing confusion, as it was perhaps also touched upon in Germany in 1933, in spite of the fascistoid or Nietzscheo-fascistoid confusion.)[12] Seen in this light, Heidegger was obviously not wrong in 1945 when he spoke of 'Western responsibility',[13] even if he is hard pressed to justify the idea that the West in 1933 was condensed into Germany alone and that the remedy to the 'crisis of the University' i.e. to the decline of science (*Wissenschaft*) was to be found in a return to the 'fundamentalism' of speculative Idealism. If the fundamentalist gesture does not necessarily dispose one towards fascism (though the urge towards founding or re-founding in fascism does seem to need closer examination), the same cannot be said of a certain 'national preference' (no other name can be given to this since Heidegger obstinately rejects the term 'nationalism').[14] If we accept that we still have to follow the trace of an 'archi-fascism', though one which becomes less and less fascist the further one follows it, it is clearly here that everything comes together. In Heideggerian terms, the question is, as I have indicated, the following: why is historial *Dasein* determined as the *Dasein* of a *people*? In more everyday political terms, we may re-write this as follows: why was Heidegger committed to the idea of a national Revolution and why did he never repudiate that commitment?

It is not quite exact to say, as I did above, that the only one of the political themes raised in 1933 to be maintained afterwards was the theme of the University. There exists a second theme, less directly political in appearance, but of decisive importance for what in Heidegger's eyes constitutes the essence of the political, i.e. for History: this is the theme of the (Greek) beginning and the relation to the beginning, in which is involved, both in the *Rectoral Address* and also afterwards, the question of a possible historical destination of German *Dasein*. It is certain that after the war, as I am not the only one to have noted, what we would now call the signifier 'German' or 'Germany' practically disappears from Heidegger's vocabulary (and even 'Europe' only figures there hesitantly, generally in composite terms such as 'Western'-European and, in general, 'the West' is substituted for 'Germany'). The political admission is clear. Yet this does not mean that the schema of historiality is modified in any respect. In one of the last lectures given by Heidegger, the Athens lecture of 1967 ('The Provenance of Art and the Destination of Thought'), which brings together powerfully the whole of Heidegger's meditation on the essence of *technē*, one may read the following, which one might also have heard in 1933 (when *technē* signified 'science') or in the years after (when *technē* referred above all to 'art'):

> We, who are members of the Academy of Arts, finding ourselves here at Athens in the presence of the Academy of Sciences in the age of scientific technology, what are we to meditate upon other than that world which lay the foundations for the arts – and the sciences – of Western Europe to begin?
>
> Certainly, for the historians, that world belongs to the past. But for History, if we experience it as what is destined for us, it remains still and will always remain a new present: something which expects of us that we approach it thoughtfully, and that we thereby put our own thinking and our own artistic creation to the test. For the beginning of a destiny is the greatest of things. From the outset, it holds everything that comes after in its power.[15]

Between 1933 and 1967, the tone has obviously changed: the pathos of meditation has been subsituted for the pathos of resolution and there is no call for a national revolution (this lecture was addressed to Greeks and the 'we' referred to Western-European man). Yet the 'message' is the same and the – now veiled – injunction is identical: the leap called for (breach and leap into the origin) is now called 'step back',[16] but it is still the destiny of Western Europe that is at stake in it. That destiny is not, admittedly, confused with that of Germany alone, but, all the same, it is still associated with the destiny of a people, the Greek people – even if as a people, they belong to the 'past'. For once again Hölderlin is called upon to reply to Hegel:

> And today? The old gods have fled. Hölderlin, who experienced this disappearance as no other poet before or since and who put it into words in such a formative manner, asks in his elegy *Brot und Wein*, dedicated to Dionysus, the god of wine:
>
>> Where, then, where do they shine, the oracles winged for far targets?
>> Delphi's asleep, – and where now is great fate to be heard?
>> (*Wo, wo leuchten sie denn, die fernhintreffenden Sprüche?*
>> *Delphi schlummert und wo tönet das grosse Geschick?*)
>
> Is there today, two and a half millennia later, an art which submits itself to such demands as art once did in Greece? And if not, from what region does the demand come to which modern art, in all its fields, responds? Its works no longer spring forth bearing the mark of the limits of a world of the popular and the national (*Ihre Werke entspringen nicht mehr den prägenden Grenzen einer Welt des Volkhaften und Nationalen*). They belong to the universality of world civilization. Their composition and organization are part of what scientific technology projects and produces. This latter has decided the mode and possibilities of man's stay in the world. The assertion that we live in a scientific world and the fact that by the appellation 'science', it is the science of nature, mathematical physics, that is meant, places emphasis upon something which is only too well-known.
>
> Given this assertion, one easily arrives at the explanation that the region in which the demands originate to which art today feels it has to respond, is none other than the scientific world.
>
> We hesitate to give our assent to this. We remain unclear about it.[17]

It is clear, then, that Heidegger never ceased to connect the possibility of History (historiality) with the possibility of a people or of the people. Which always also meant conjointly, as we know, with the possibility of an art (a *Dichtung*), a language and a myth (a *Sage*, i.e. a relation with the gods). The Athens lecture closes on these lines from Pindar:

> Longer than deeds liveth the word, whatsoever it be that the tongue, by the favour of the Graces, draweth forth from the depth of the mind.

I do not know if this can be accounted 'archi-fascism'. I doubt it very much, even though all kinds of neo-fascisms have taken over this thematics without any appparently insurmountable difficulties. [18] What can clearly be seen, on the other hand, is that:

1   this national-popular position, which both explains the guarded commitment to Nazism and the (national-revolutionary) revolutionary radicalism of the discourse of the 1930s, is the very position from which Heidegger denounced fascism (and fascisms). Undoubtedly, this denunciation also ultimately encompasses Marxism (communism) and 'Americanism' too: all the planet's metaphysico-political systems are products of nihilism and are merely the result of its definitive (or indefinite) installation. The denunciation of fascism is, however, the more radical in that fascism, in so far as it derived its authority from (or based itself upon) a national revolution, contained the possibility of being misapprehended. This is clearly what Heidegger never forgave it;

2   in spite of all his 'nostalgic' or even genuinely 'reactionary' weaknesses, for which his protestations of non-hostility towards (modern) technology do not really compensate, Heidegger re-opened philosophically, in the wake of Nietzsche and Romanticism, questions which the Marxist *vulgate* that prevailed in Europe during the first twenty years after the war (the years of the anti-fascist 'consensus') regarded as completely obsolete, but which we can today see to be unavoidable: these are the questions of peoples (or nations), languages and religions. The way Heidegger worked these through, particularly on the basis of the problem of language, is vastly superior to anything the past century – or in the first half of this one the conflict between nationalism and internationalism (between 'Right' and 'Left' romanticisms) – might have contributed to the topic; moreover, this is one reason why we must not abandon these questions to a new *vulgate* (neo-this or neo-that) that is eager to revive the past century or the one before – to restore the Europe of *Kultur* or of the Enlightenment – and totally incapable of rising to the level of Heidegger's questioning. One hardly needed to be clairvoyant to ask oneself between 1956 and 1968 whether Marx or Nietzsche had been right, just a little more than a hundred years before, about the future of the world. One has felt equal cause for concern, since then, at seeing

Marxism – used in the interim to justify any and every kind of third-worldism – quite simply 'dropped' (without examination, and, as they say, without a second thought), at a time when the analysis of the 'commodity-form', – now the *only* form in our 'world' – is increasingly pertinent. It was not merely sufficient in either case to allow oneself to be guided by Heidegger's questions – this is never enough – but one did have to take those questions seriously and try to understand what had led such a thinking as his – not only, once again, the greatest of our time, but also the most powerful – to move from the fascist positions of 1933 to the problematizing of technology.

None of this is meant to 'excuse' Heidegger, nor even less to pardon him. I shall repeat once again that his silence after the war – his silence on the Extermination – is unpardonable. And all the more unpardonable in that, when he wanted to, Heidegger could say something. As evidence, let us cite this solemn opening to his lecture of 20 June 1952 (after his readmission to teaching):

> Ladies and Gentlemen,
> Today in Freiburg, the exhibition 'The Prisoners of War Speak' has opened. I urge you to visit it. In order to hear this silent voice and never more to let it leave your inward ear.
>   Thought is faithful thought (*Denken ist Andenken*). But faithful thought is something other than a fleeting actualization of the past. Faithful thought considers what affects us. We are not yet in the proper space to reflect upon freedom, nor even to speak of it, so long as we *also* close our eyes to this annihilation of freedom.[19]

This was all he said then on the *disaster*. This single word deploring what occurred in Germany alone (or, rather, 'Germany' alone) and irreversibly casting suspicion on the very parsimonious expressions of regret that one might have cited in his favour. (Thus when he spoke of *Unheil*, what or who in fact was he thinking of?) The question is not – though one hears it posed often enough – what he could have said, what word or phrase would have been able to do justice to such an event? If no word or phrase could do that, it was simple to say so – though doubtless too simple for the thinking (*Denken*) and the recollection (*Andenken*) of the simple. It is not even a question of knowing why he said nothing: it is only too clear that he was concerned above all to clear Germany of the charge against it and that deep down, he disavowed nothing or almost nothing. But the question is: was the silence – the safeguarding of Germany – worth the risk for thought itself, of a (confessionless) confession of complicity with crime?

It is this question which, 'for a thousand years' (let us remember also the reality of this historical calculation) the thinker's thinking leaves open. The ultimate paradox is that it is preserved, as memorial, in a poem by a Jewish poet, which is entitled as the reader will remember – and we must remember – *Todtnauberg*.

NOTES

1 In January 1963, *Diskus*, the Frankfurt student newspaper, published an open letter to Adorno signed by Claus Ch. Schroeder. In that letter he was asked to confirm that he had indeed been the author of a review article that appeared in June 1934 in *Die Musik*, the 'official journal of the Reich youth organization', in which he had given a particularly favourable reception to the song-cycle *The Standard of the Persecuted*, by Herbert Müntzel, which was based on a collection of poems by Baldur von Schirach (which was, incidentally, dedicated to 'the Führer, Adolf Hitler'). Adorno's notice in fact contained particularly incriminating declarations of allegiance: Müntzel's cycle, 'by virtue of the choice of Schirach's poems' stood out, Adorno said, 'as being consciously National Socialist'; and he also spoke of the search 'for the image of a new romanticism' which he related to Goebbels's 'romantic realism'. Claus Chr. Schroeder simply asked him how the author of *Minima moralia* could, 'before Auschwitz, have approved such monstrous songs' and how he could, consequently, claim the right to condemn 'all those who had been accessories in what had happened in Germany since 1934', reminding Adorno, for example, of his writings on Heidegger.

In his reply, which appeared in the same number of *Diskus*, Adorno acknowledged that he was the author of the notice and said that he regretted 'from the bottom of his heart' having written it, while explaining, with some embarrassment, that these declarations had to be seen in context (these 'crudely tactical' declarations had to be understood as *captationes benevolentiae*) aimed at assisting the new music to 'survive the winter of the Third Reich'). He admitted that he had committed an error of judgement so far as the situation in 1933–4 was concerned and had thought it necessary at that stage to save 'those things that could still be saved'. But, he added: 'I would, however, be willing to submit myself to a fair-minded tribunal and let it decide whether the offending statements weigh very heavily in relation to my work and life as a whole.' These words were in fact a commentary upon the statement that immediately preceded them: 'it ought to be impossible for anyone who inspects my work in its continuity to compare me with Heidegger, whose philosophy is fascist right down to its innermost components (*dessen Philosophie bis in ihre innersten Zellen faschistisch ist*)'.

Commenting upon this reply, Hannah Arendt will write to Karl Jaspers on 4 July 1966 that she found it 'indescribably distressing'.

(Adorno's letter is published in its entirety in the editorial Postface to volumes 5 and 6 of *Musikalische Schriften* (Suhrkamp, 1976), pp. 637–8. Hannah Arendt's letter appears in Hannah Arendt – Karl Jaspers, *Briefwechsel* (Munich, Piper, 1985), p. 679. The circumstances are recalled by the editors Lotte Köhler and Hans Saner in a footnote to p. 829. I thank Françoise Dastur and Alex Garcia Düttman who provided me with these documents.)

2   Professor Richard Wisser, Interview with Heidegger, broadcast 24 September 1969 by ZDF, Germany. [This translation from the French transcription: C.T.]

3   From 'The Thinker as Poet' (*'Aus der Erfahrung des Denkens'*) in *Poetry, Language and Thought* trans. A Hofstadter (New York, Harper and Row, 1975), p. 9.

4   This emerges in particular from Jean-Luc Nancy's analyses in *la Communauté désoeuvrée* and *L'Expérience de la liberté*. (forthcoming)

5   Karl Löwith, *Mein Leben in Deutschland vor und nach 1933, Ein Bericht*, p. 32 ff.

6   See my own essay, 'La transcendence finie/t dans la politique', *L'Imitation des modernes* (Paris, Galilée, 1986).

7   'L'Ontologie politique de Martin Heidegger', *Actes de la recherche* (November, 1975). (Now republished with additional material in book format (Paris, Minuit, 1988), CT).

8   Cf. The Letter to the de-Nazification Committee at Freiburg Univerisity:

I was already opposed in this same way to the National Socialist world-view doctrine in 1933–34; I did, however, believe that the movement could be spiritually directed on to other paths and I felt such an attempt could be combined with the social and overall political tendencies of the movement. I believed that Hitler, after he assumed responsibility for the *whole* people in 1933, would grow beyond the party and its doctrine and everything would come together, through a renovation and a rallying, in an assumption of Western responsibility. This belief proved erroneous, as I recognized from the events of 30 June 1934. It had, however, brought me to a half-way house position (*Zwischenstellung*) in that I accepted the Social and the National (not the Nationalist) elements and rejected the intellectual/spiritual (*geistig*) and metaphysical foundations as expressed in the biologism of the party doctrine, because the Social and the National were not in my view existentially connected to the biological – racist world-view doctrine . . .

Einige Auszüge aus einem Brief an den Vorsitzenden des politischen Reinigungsausschusses, Karl A Moehling, *Martin Heidegger and the Nazi Party: An Examination* (Ph.D dissertation, Northern Illinois University, 1972, Ann Arbor Microfilms, 72 – 29, 319), pp. 270 – 1.

9   Moreover, fascism itself is directly and explicitly attacked in many of his writings from these years. In para. 27 of 'Overcoming Metaphysics', for example, Gentile's *actualismo* is denounced. I refer the reader here to the work of Charles Alunni on Gentile and the philosophy of fascism (forthcoming).

10 Quoted from the French translation of Wisser's interview, *Cahiers de L'Herne: Heidegger*, p. 93.

11 In Moehling, *Martin Heidegger and the Nazi Party*, p. 269.

12 This was also the case in Mussolini's Italy where one of the earliest and most far-reaching reforms was Gentile's reform of the school and university systems. Perhaps since Condorcet, modern politics has distinguished itself by the priority it accords to Science and schools.

13 Letter to the Rector of Freiburg University (4 November 1945), Moehling *Martin Heidegger and the Nazi Party*, p. 265.

14 Cf. the letter cited above (n. 8). This rejection is constant in Heidegger, on grounds of principle.

15 'The Provenance of Art and the Destination of Thought'. Translated from the version which appeared in the *Cahiers de l'Herne*, p. 84.

16 'It is necessary to take a step backwards. Backwards, towards what? Back towards the beginning that announced itself to us when we

referred to the goddess Athena (in order to grasp Greek art in its provenance, P.L-L.). But this step back does not mean that we should in some way or other revive the world of ancient Greece and that thought should seek refuge among the pre-Socratics.

"Step back" means that thought recoils before world civilization and, taking its distance from it, but in no sense denying it, introduces itself into what was still to remain unthought at the beginning of Western thought, but which is also already named there, and thus disclosed in advance, to our thought' (ibid., p. 90).

The step back thus obeys the same logic of repetition (of the greatness of the Greek beginning) that is at work in the *Rectoral Address*.

17 Ibid., p. 87 [I have followed Lacoue-Labarthe's 'modified' transla-
tion closely here. The verse is Michael Hamburger's version from
Friedrich Hölderlin, *Poems and Fragments* (Cambridge University
Press, 1980), p. 247: C.T.]

18 This is the case, for example, in a number of the review *Nouvelle
Ecole* 37 (Spring, 1982) entitled 'Lectures de Heidegger' ('Readings
of Heidegger') and containing in particular an article by Robert
Stenckers ('Conception de l'homme et Révolution conservatrice:
Heidegger et son temps') and a text by Guillaume Faye and Patrick
Rizzi ('Pour en finir avec le nihilisme'). To say that this type of
avowed neo-fascism takes over Heidegger's political thematics
'without apparent difficulty' does not mean that it does so without
dishonesty. I shall say nothing of the more minor offences; lines
taken from the elegy *Brot und Wein* are attributed to the hymn, *Aus
dem Motivkreis der Titanen*, since the former is presumably considered too Christian in inspiration (p. 44); or, employing the
opposite tactic, the *Rectoral Address* is referred to by the periphrasis,
'In one of his lectures on science . . . (Heidegger says . . .)' etc. These
minor dishonesties are legion and are never without their significance. But the basic dishonesty clearly lies in the 'reading': the
operation (which at bottom is one of pure and simple 'recuperation')
is only possible on condition that one projects (back) upon the
Heideggerian discourse of the 1930's Nietzschean philosophemes
(will to power, overman [Übermensch], Appollinian and Diony-
sian, etc.) which Heidegger made every effort to delimit. All in all,
simply by not reading his *Nietzsche*, one can obtain a fascist
Heidegger.

19 *Was heißt denken?* (Tübingen, Max Niemeyer Verlag, 1961), p. 159.
    [My translation; the passage is not translated in the Wieck and Glenn
    Gray translation and I have followed Lacoue-Labarthe's French
    version closely: C.T.]

Appendix   On Victor Farias's Book, *Heidegger et le nazisme*

It is generally thought to be rather perilous to sit in judgement in an affair in which one is personally involved. I am, none the less, going to venture to do so. It is, after all, merely a test of honesty.

I had just finished correcting the proofs of this book when I learned through the press, somewhat belatedly, of the publication in France of Victor Farias's book, *Heidegger et le nazisme* (Paris, Verdier, 1987). Apparently this was causing quite a stir: there was talk of a 'bombshell', a 'literary sensation', a 'damning indictment'. Reviews of the book – at least the ones I managed to find – did not, however, mention any new findings that were not previously known. But, by its manner of presenting the 'Heidegger affair' and also by the vocabulary it employed ('militancy', 'activism', 'continuity of membership', etc.) and its stressing of the incomplete and even downright mendacious character of Heidegger's 'testamentary' declarations and explanations (particularly the famous *Spiegel* interview), it was apparent that this book, which received praise for its historian's impartiality and absence of hatred (it was pointed out that Farias had been a student of Heidegger's, not of course that this proves very much), offered a version of the affair which at least merited serious examination, and might well, indeed, lead to some serious revising of the historical record. We knew (at least the better informed of us knew) that it was probable Heidegger had considerably played down the reality and extent of his commitment and presented a particularly euphemistic version of the political compromise in which he had been involved. In any case, that much was clearly evident on a simple reading of the texts in which he sought to justify himself. It was, however, rather more difficult to take the further step and accept that he had lied about the *meaning* of his commitment to – and his 'break' with (or at least his withdrawal from) – the movement, that is to say about the essential question, about what connected that commitment and that withdrawal with his thought. Deep down, everyone knows this very well. Now that step, in my opinion, remains impossible. In any case, reading this book has not convinced me this is not the case.

Victor Farias's thesis can be stated in a few propositions which I shall here rehearse briefly:

(1)   By virtue of his social and regional origin (Swabia and, more generally, Catholic and conservative southern Germany), his education (also Catholic), the company he kept and his tastes, the influences upon him and his intellectual training, Heidegger was profoundly marked by an ideological tradition which is one of the sources, and will be one of the components, of the National Socialist revolution, as is attested by his 'emblematic' (and stubborn) attachment to the baroque preacher Abraham a Sancta Clara, 'a seventeenth-century representative of an authoritarian, anti-semitic and ultra-nationalist tradition'. Consequently, if one attempts to situate the pre-1933 Heidegger from a political point of view, one has not only to place him 'on the Right', but to see him as one of the potential partisans of a particularly hard and aggressive extremist national populism which will in fact assert a degree of dominance for several months in 1933 and 1934, but which will not survive – or will only partially survive – the various compromises struck with the bourgeoisie, the Church and Capital. This is the case for the author of *Sein und Zeit* and the book on Kant. Which is to say that it is also the case for the participant in the Davos Colloquium on Kantianism, which saw him pitted fiercely against Cassirer, the prominent representative of the Jewish 'intelligentsia' (or academy).

(2)   His commitment in 1933 is total, unreserved and brutal, and it is a commitment to the most revolutionary positions of the 'movement' – those of the SA. Heidegger's desire in accepting (or in soliciting through the good offices of others) the post of Rector

is to reform the University from top to bottom (a project which we know he had harboured ever since his Inaugural Address of 1929 at Freiburg, 'What is Metaphysics?') by enlisting the support, almost exclusively, of the students following, if one will, the logic of a sort of fascist May 68. Heidegger throws himself body and soul into this task – or adventure. Enjoying unlimited powers by virtue of the *Führerprinzip*, he makes a great number of public declarations and conducts many seminars at 'indoctrination camps', takes administrative measures intended to achieve the 'co-ordination' ('Gleichschaltung') of the University, makes all kinds of 'political' contacts with intellectuals favourable to the regime and very quickly becomes one of the movement's outstanding figures. At this period, he is a convinced and enthusiastic National Socialist. He even goes so far as to expose disloyal colleagues. If he fails and if he is forced, a year later, to resign, this is because the tendency on which he based his power – the SA tendency which was dominant in the student associations – is being defeated, as is attested in June 1934 by the elimination of Röhm. It is his 'radicalism' which forces him to withdraw. But withdrawing from the movement is not the same as breaking with it.

(3)   A wealth of documentation proves that Heidegger did in fact continue to be 'politically active' in favour of the regime after 1934. Not only did he not hand in his party card (he kept it until 1945), but he contributed to several plans for university reform within the Reich (*Dozentenakademie des deutschen Reiches, Academie für deutsches Recht, Deutsche Hochschule für Politik*). He was obviously the target of the official ideologues of the SS tendency (Rosenberg, Krieck, Bäumler) and as such he suffered several petty annoyances. But he remained highly regarded in Goebbels' ministry, had powerful allies in fascist Italy (the *Duce* himself went so far as to intervene on his behalf) and, contrary to what he would say in later years, he was neither forbidden to publish nor was he excised from the galaxy of the regime's major thinkers. He was also allowed to participate in congresses abroad, his students were not persecuted, his teaching was not put under surveillance and he was not apparently excluded from the University (to be called up again) in 1944. All that can be found to say in his favour,

so to speak, is that in his teaching and certain of his public declarations, he took a very clear stand against the dominant tendency within the party and the regime, that is against what Farias insists upon calling – and I cannot help but admit that this leaves me non-plussed – the Hitlerian 'deviationism' of National Socialism (once this nuance has been established, it does in fact become possible to speak of a 'continuity' in Heidegger's commitment . . .).

(4)   After the war and the defeat of Germany, Heidegger repudiated nothing; he stubbornly refused to retract anything and continued to nurture hopes of a 'spiritual' renaissance of the West (of Europe) radiating out from Germany – if not indeed from Swabia and the Alemannic *Heimat*. Above all, he took pains to give out an 'honourable' version of his political involvement and to reinvent a 'political virginity' for himself, using Beaufret and Char to give him respectability. For this reason, his justificatory writings are purely and simply lies. They are, in any case, of little weight by comparison with the terrible silence he maintained concerning the Extermination (the Shoah) and his return to old and dubious examples (Abraham a Sancta Clara).

This argument seems soundly based. Certain well-known German works had already taken the historical investigation and the exploration of the archives quite some way (the work of Hugo Ott and Bernd Martin in particular). Victor Farias completes their work on several points and simply takes stock of – or seems to be taking stock of – the whole question on the basis of the currently available documents (but so many things remain in the shadows, beginning with the Heidegger archive). One might just be a little surprised that he makes no use of recent material (the Heidegger – Kästner correspondence for example, which would have enlightened him as to how the interview granted to *Der Spiegel* came about, or Löwith's memoirs); or that he makes nothing of the tribulations in Heidegger's relations with Hannah Arendt, which are surely very instructive and which are also a part of this history. Just when was this book written exactly? Nevertheless, the impression given is that this is a serious work by a scrupulous historian.

Sadly, this is only an impression. The book is profoundly unjust and I even consider it – and I am weighing my words carefully here – dishonest. Moreover, in view of this, I am not surprised to see mentioned in the author's acknowledgements the name of Jean-Pierre Faye, who distinguished himself some twenty-five years ago by a rather surprising presentation/translation of Heidegger's political declarations taken from Schneeberger's anthology. This is indeed true devotion to a cause; and it produces the unpleasant impression that this is a 'put-up job', of the type we see only too often on our intellectual 'scene'.

Let us attempt to examine the matter with a minimum of probity.

First of all, it goes without saying that even if I do not share without (philosphical and political) reservations in the 'democratic consensus' which seems to reign at present – to say nothing of 'juridical humanism' – Nazism is in my opinion, as in that of Farias, Faye and many others, an *absolutely* vile phenomenon both in its goals and its results – without question the most grave – by a long way – that the West has known (i.e. that it has produced). My position is perfectly clear on this subject and I have explained it sufficiently in the preceding chapters. Obviously, it is not this point that need detain us here. Discussion may, however, be opened not on the evaluation of Nazism, but on *thinking* Nazism (after all, the phenomenon was not born out of nothing, but came from us, 'good Europeans that we are') and thinking through its stunning success, its power of seduction, its project and its victories etc., and above all thinking what it might have represented for intellectuals of the period, not all of whom – far from it – were imbeciles or opportunists. Why, in the twenties and thirties was there such a rejection of democracy on both Right and Left? And why this theme, which was by no means peculiar to Heidegger, and which went back deep into German tradition, of the distress (*Not*) of Germany? Why this preoccupation with the nation? Why was there such certainty both within Germany and outside it, that Europe was heading for catastrophe? And why such anxiety, shared just as much by Valéry and Bergson, Blanchot and Husserl, Bataille and Heidegger, Benjamin and Malraux, to mention but a few? These are so many questions – but there are many others – which Farias's book does not even raise, yet which it is essential to ask if we are to try to gain even a remote understanding of what happened – and certainly may happen again. To regard the monstrous nature of Nazism merely as an accepted fact is a grave error – both politically and philosophically – if it means one feels one may dispense with questioning it.

Having said this – and this also goes without saying – I am not for a moment trying to seek the least indulgence for Heidegger. Reading his texts, I am convinced that his political commitment was neither accidental nor a product of error and that it must be considered as a wrong – in the sense, initially but not exclusively – of an offence against thought. This is why, as regards its strictly documentary complexity, there is nothing to complain of in Farias's book: the facts cited are, so far as I know, incontestable – and others could very certainly be added. There remains a great deal of work yet for the historians. I even agree that Farias is right to insist on Heidegger's revolutionary 'radicalism', even though I have considerable reservations about the conclusions he draws from this. Undeniably, Heidegger went a long way in his commitment (much too far for the Nazis themselves); undeniably also, he did not disavow very much as regards the basic issues, i.e. as regards the 'truth and inner greatness of this movement'. But then why omit to mention what he did explicitly disavow? For example, in the *Spiegel* interview, all the public declarations of 1933–4 except the *Rektoratsrede*. After all, it is rare enough to find Heidegger showing remorse. It is to say the least inelegant not to take it into account, or, which amounts to much the same, only to take into account those parts of his posthumous declarations which provide material that can be used against him. Surely the affair itself is serious enough without having to add to it . . .

In reality, the three reasons which lead me to suspect this work are of a quite other order than the factual.

I shall pass over some patently dishonest procedures and a number of errors. For example, among the dishonest procedures, one may cite the technique of adding the adjective 'Aryan' to every occurrence of the word 'People' when translating the 'Appeal to Labour Service' (pp. 135–6). On page 175, it becomes clear that this is a way of translating the notorious term '*völkisch*' and one can also see where the manoeuvre comes from. (I have no means of verifying this, but I seem to recognize here the translation by Jean-Pierre Faye which I mentioned above.) On the following page, however, one can see that when Heidegger wanted to say 'Aryan', he said '*Arier*' like everyone else . . .

As for the errors, the most obvious is the one that concerns Abraham a Sancta Clara's phrase that is quoted by Heidegger in his homage of 1964 (which is, incidentally, far from being Heidegger's 'last text'): 'Our peace is as far from war as Sachsenhausen is from Frankfurt.' Is this, asks Farias, a Freudian slip? No one could fail to know at this time that Sachsenhausen was 'one of the most sinister of the concentration camps built by the Third Reich' and that Frankfurt is the 'headquarters of the tribunal that has responsibility for investigating the crimes perpetrated at Auschwitz'. The connection is quite clear and since everyone knows Abraham a Sancta Clara is or was a convinced anti-semite, it is but a short step from the slip to an 'unconscious retraction' and from there to a deliberate 'provocation'. We might in passing note that Farias has not for a moment asked himself why Heidegger had never mentioned Abraham a Sancta Clara's anti-semitism, either in 1910 or 1964, since he holds his 'virtuosity' in manipulating quotations in such high esteem. But he is out of luck here. As Joseph Hanimann revealed in his column in the *Frankfurter Allgemeine Zeitung* of 28 October 1987, there is no connection whatever between the suburb of Frankfurt and the concentration camp of the same name.

I come then to my three reasons for suspecting this work.

The first concerns its rhetoric and, what I would call its 'staging' of the events. The book's rhetoric consists essentially in translating into strictly (narrowly) political terms the least (and not only the least) of Heidegger's actions: If Heidegger joins the Party in 1933, he becomes an 'activist'. If he does too much (or even much too much) during his rectorship, he is a 'zealous activist': all his pedagogical initiatives have to do with 'indoctrination' and all his administrative measures with 'co-ordination' (*Gleichschaltung*). If he takes part, after his resignation (from the rectorship) in the formulation of institutional projects (three of these, and this hardly takes us beyond 1934), then he continued to be an 'activist'.

As proof of this, the fact that he did not hand in his party card.
(But where and when is he supposed to have claimed that he did?
The only declaration of his I know of on this subject explained
that, since one of his sons was on the Russian front, it had not
seemed opportune to resign in a glare of publicity.) Farias lumps
together in this same category of 'activism' – under the overblown
title, 'Heidegger et les appareils d'Etat' ('Heidegger and the State
Apparatuses') – the review of an article (which is, admittedly, very
eloquent) by Frau Heidegger, one or two university intrigues
(quite normal as it happens: they simply concern appointments to
university chairs), the 1936 lectures on the work of art (and it is
surely no minor weakness that no actual reading is made of these –
not even in their 'political' dimensions), Mussolini's intervention
with Goebbels – and against the advice of the Rosenberg Office –
in favour of the publication in Ernesto Grassi's *Yearbook* (*Geistige
Überlieferung*) of Heidegger's text on Plato ('*Platons Lehre von der
Wahrheit*', – what was Mussolini's concern in all this?). The final
straw is a chapter on 'Heidegger à Prague (1940) et à Munich
(1941)' (pp. 269–70) in which we learn from a document (in
actual fact a report from the Rosenberg *Amt*) which is supposed to
show 'the ambivalence of Heidegger's political position in the
forties (total acceptance of the regime and rejection of its concrete
policies)', that a certain Kurt Schilling, a professor of philosophy
at Prague (in occupied territory and therefore under special
surveillance), conducted courses in which 'reference was made' to
'Heideggerian concepts'.

I accept that it can be very useful – and even healthy – to take
certain Heideggerian statements literally, to be on one's guard for
euphemisms and observe the greatest caution towards a rhetoric
(Heidegger's) that is governed by the refusal of the ontically
obvious. But, none the less, one has to know what one is doing: to
say – and this is a famous example (virtually an anthology piece) –
that Heidegger's ontological variations upon 'staying' and 'dwelling' are nothing but poorly disguised petty-bourgeois truisms
about the housing crisis has never got anyone very far. I fear that
in describing Heidegger's political commitment Farias is falling
into the same error. The fact that Heidegger would probably have
rejected the term 'activist', as he rejected the term 'political' in

1935 (The *Introduction to Metaphysics*), raises an enormous question. To evade that question, by adopting the rather simple stance of an 'external critique' and arguing that one has to 'call a spade a spade', is not necessarily to set things back in their right place. One may lay emphasis upon Heidegger's compromises (he acknowledged them – or at least certain of them – himself), but one must also take the measure of the meaning Heidegger intended to give, before and after 1934, to his political involvement. Farias's political 'translation' does not come anywhere near doing this.

This is all the more serious in that the said translation is reinforced by a 'cumulative' presentation, which generates more confusion than enlightenment. It is fairly well known that in a National Socialist State all office-holders normally had to belong to the Party. It is also clear that nothing could be done (neither a university appointment nor the slightest reform project or publication) without the Party being involved, without it exercising surveillance or issuing directives, and without more or less secret reports being circulated etc. This is part of what 'totalitarianism' means, even when, as in the Third Reich, it gives rise to extreme confusion as a result of the rivalries between different authorities, administrations, services, factions or pressure groups, persons etc. For Farias, however, the sole criterion of political classification, once the great SA–SS distinction has been made, is Party membership. I am not saying that this is an insignificant or neutral phenomenon (non-membership of the Party certainly had a very clear meaning). But when I see that for page after page we are spared no party membership number, no *Gau* reference, no rank, grade or distinction in the SS, I ask myself what image or impression the author is in fact trying to create, if it is not the following: that Heidegger, himself a Nazi, is in all his actions, in all his relationships whether within or outside the university, in his work and in his friendships (even in his marriage) surrounded only by Nazis, all of whom are virtually identical in as much as they are all Nazis. In the end, particularly since Farias works fairly systematically to minimize the hostility of the Rosenberg clan (and the significance of this hostility), it becomes difficult, so powerful is the 'shopping list' effect, to see what difference there might be between Bäumler and Otto, Schadewalt and Professor Heyse, the Mayor of Freiburg and the Minister of Education etc. etc. Now, to take just this one example, if one reads *Volk im Werden* (Krieck's review) and the two or three numbers of *Geistige Überlieferung (Spiritual Tradition)* edited by Grassi, Otto and Reinhardt, it is impossible to confuse the two. Grassi was certainly a fascist (as for Otto and Reinhardt, I do not know if they had party cards), but the Rosenberg *Amt* was certainly not mistaken when it placed *Geistige Überlieferung* under surveillance and sought to distance Heidegger from it. He no doubt did have powerful allies in fascist Italy, but that did not prevent him from being so ungrateful as publicly to criticize *actualismo*, the official philosophy of fascism. Should this be put down as part of the struggle against 'revisionism'? Or is it a form of 'relativization', for this is the delicate euphemism Farias uses when he can clearly see that he is dealing after all, in Heidegger's writings or lectures (at least those which he deigns to look at), with a *critique* of Nazism.

My second reason for being suspicious of this book is that, following this same peculiar style of presentation – though this time with regard to texts (and this seems to me much more serious) – Farias constantly employs a technique of guilt by association.

The intention is always, of course, to cast light upon the context and at the beginning, one cannot see (or can see only imperfectly) the significance of the manoeuvre. But in this case the accumulation effect is ultimately self-defeating. By wishing to prove too much ... One is amazed, for example, at the beginning of the book by the clumsiness of Farias's presentation of Heidegger's first text on Abraham a Sancta Clara (pp. 39–55): a long biography of Abraham a Sancta Clara reminding us of the anti-semitic tradition in which he was situated and which he perpetuated, an analysis of his influence on the anti-semitic currents in Austria and South Germany, a history of the Social Christian movement and its leader, Karl Lueger, a description of the festival commemorating him for which Heidegger wrote his text (all the foregoing was necessary, says Farias at the beginning of this piece, because in actual fact the commemoration could not have taken place without the funds provided by the Vienna City Council, i.e. by Lueger), a presentation and political analysis of Heidegger's text, a note on his textual sources, (Bertsche's *Auswahl* which, we might add, remains discreet on the matter of Abraham a Sancta Clara's anti-semitism), presentation of the review in which Heidegger's text will appear (accompanied by a reference to the obituary of Lueger – an emotive homage to his anti-semitism – which appeared in an earlier number), an account of the local newspaper's account of the ceremonies, and, lastly, an analysis of the conflict between integrist and modernist Catholics 'which Heidegger had made the main theme of his contribution'. There is a little too much of 'race, milieu and moment' in this, as in all the long biographical account that forms the first part of the book ('Des années de jeunesse au rectorat' – (1889–1933)), but these details are obviously relatively useful: Heidegger, like anyone else, was not born out of nothing and his life cannot simply be situated within the philosphical tradition alone (that is why his – customary – disavowal of the biographical had its reasons). The people he chose to frequent and those whom he agreed (or did not refuse) to mix with undoubtedly left their mark upon him, and it is useful to know what his most spontaneous sympathies were. 'Tell me who your friends are . . .' is not a bad rule and the time had doubtless come to 'situate' Heidegger politically. But was it really necessary to conflate Heidegger's discourse with that of those around him, to fill up his own silences (on anti-semitism in particular) with other people's remarks and to give rein systematically, over more than 300 pages, to a kind of *law of contamination* which ends up producing the impression that Heidegger is in fact reponsible for things that he did not say? This is a strange conception of 'textual authority' and it becomes quite staggering when Heidegger's text, re-situated in this way within its 'context', is not even quoted (I was going to say 'commented upon' , but that would clearly be asking too much). This is the case, for example, when mention is made of the circumstances surrounding the publication of *Andenken* in 1943 in the collection published to celebrate the hundredth anniversary of Hölderlin's death, a collection which was enthusiastically welcomed – how could it have been otherwise? – by the regime. When one understands the tremendous significance Hölderlin had for Heidegger after 1935–6, this is outrageous.

This brings me to my third reason for suspecting this book: *Farias quite simply does not read Heidegger's text.* Including what can be extracted, though with some difficulty, as the most directly political of texts. Admittedly, Farias quotes abundantly, gives résumés and accounts of writings both by Heidegger and by others. But, on the one hand, his philosphical understanding of Heidegger leaves one quite flabbergasted. (You only have to read, among other purple passages, the beginning of chapter 4, part 3 (pp. 291–2) on 'Heidegger's thinking in his later years': a piece of writing which would be unacceptable from a sixth-former in France. Victor Farias has put it about that he was a student of Heidegger's, but, as Jacques Derrida says, 'These things happen'.[1]) On the other hand, and perhaps most importantly, Farias maintains a systematic silence on the texts in which Heidegger 'engages' with National Socialism (in particular) and with politics (in general). Heidegger devotes more than four years of his teaching between 1936 and 1941 to 'delimiting' Nietzsche's metaphysics and openly contesting its 'diversion' into biologism and the use that is made of it by the official racist ideology: Farias hardly touches on a word of this. During his lifetime, after the war, Heidegger publishes the texts written and some of the lectures delivered in the 'dark years', the ones I imagine he must have thought best fitted to illuminate his thinking – if not his attitude. These include, for example, the series of notes written between 1936 and 1946 known by the title 'Overcoming Metaphysics' (translated in *The End of Philosophy*) and, as regards lecture courses, alongside the two volumes of Nietszsche, the *Introduction to Metaphysics* (from 1935) and the *Schelling* (from 1936), which both contain extremely clear remarks directed against the confusion of values, *Weltanschauungen* and lived experience maintained by the official philosophy, as well as against anti-semitic discrimination in the sphere of thought (in relation to Spinoza, for example). Farias says nothing of this. And he says nothing about the lectures published since Heidegger's death in 1976, particularly his lectures on Hölderlin, which have a crucial political significance (or rather which probably contain all Heidegger's 'political' thinking). One of two things must be true. Either all these texts, given the strictly unverifiable conditions of their publication and the closure of the Heidegger archives, are crude forgeries or at best 'rectified' texts (but at no point does Farias mention the problems posed by the continuing publication of the *Gesamtausgabe*) or they may be considered, whether or not they were published by Heidegger, part of the Heideggerian *corpus* and if this is so, they cannot then be left out of account: this is a matter of the most elementary honesty in dealing with a subject of this order. Where is Heidegger's 'philosophy', or rather, where is what he thought, if not in his texts? And what is on trial: Heidegger's thought or something else? If there is a 'Heidegger affair' – and though his silent complicity is terrifying, to the best of my knowledge, no 'crime against humanity' is involved in that affair – it is because of 'Heidegger's thought'. We are not talking about any old person being politically compromised, about some teacher or other or party member so and so. If this were the case, we would not even spend five minutes on the subject. We are talking about the greatest thinker of our age. It is in his thought therefore that the question of political responsibility is posed. By virtually ignoring that thought, by not reading or only half understanding the texts, by not taking into account *all* the facts (it is not only party card numbers that count, or anecdotes, but *all* the texts, including indeed those of others, though did Farias ever think to compare these, to differentiate between them?), one can indeed speak of an 'unconditional commitment to the general stock of National Socialist ideas' (p. 289). But it is outrageous to do so.

Let me say once again that I am not in favour of minimizing Heidegger's political responsibility, as has too often been the case in the past. I simply feel that one has to preserve a certain correctness, understanding this term both in the sense of fairness and of exactitude. We must therefore judge on the basis of the evidence. And visibly this is not done by 'lumping together' documents that are heterogeneous both in their – philosphical and political – meaning and importance. There is no doubt (and this is already serious – or 'disappointing' enough) that Heidegger be-longed to the Nazi party, that his positions were radical and that he subsequently became disaffected, without that disaffection becoming so great as to cause him to make a clean break with the movement. It still remains, however, to understand exactly what he was committing himself to, what gave rise to his disaffection and what it was that he did not deny. One is clearly not going to achieve this by referring to post-1934 Hitlerism as 'deviationism'. Nor by ascribing to Heidegger, however deviously, certain statements, ideas (or ideologemes) or thoughts when all his work shows that he could not for a moment have accepted them, or claimed them as his own. The same goes for his – perplexing – post-war silence. What kind of solidarity does this manifest, and with what (the regime? Germany? Europe?)? The only hope of finding an answer to these questions – or even the beginnings of an answer (the 'case' is after all very difficult) – lies in our facing up to a rigorous reading of the texts.

The annoying thing about this 'unconditional commitment' thesis is that is is presented as the product of scrupulous historical research and we know what authority history enjoys among almost all our contemporaries. The outrageous, or (distressingly simple) nature of this thesis is, I am certain, of no consequence – except perhaps for the army of anti-Heideggerians who are in any case already convinced and have had no need to wait for Farias's book before feeling they could denounce any acknowledgement – even the most vigilant, critical or circumspect acknowledgement – of Heidegger's thought as 'fascist'. Even the stir Farias's book has created in 'the media' (where it has had a disproportionate response, considering the quality of the work) is not (too) worrying: real work (there has been some on this topic and there will be more in the future) always becomes known where it has to be known, and the true questions always get through in the end.

What would be worrying, however, would be for the affair to be considered 'settled' at least for a time, and for a *doxa* to form that regarded the matter as closed. We can already see the 'Is it still alright to read Heidegger?' articles doing the rounds. If this were to be the effect of this book (dissuading people from reading and questioning), it would be a catastrophe. But it would be sad to despair of people's capacity to read . . .

Berkeley, November 1987

NOTES

Except for a few modifications, this is the text of an article which first appeared in the *Journal littéraire*.
1. 'Heidegger, l'enfer des philosophes'. Interview published in *Le Nouvel Observateur*, 6–12 November 1987. I should like to say that I agree totally with Jacques Derrida's comments on Farias's book.

Index